Also by
E. Wayne McLaughlin

———

Whatever 2005

The Three Pigs of Jesus 2006

Many Rooms, Many Windows 2010

*Down on the Farm with
Raymond and Dorothy Crawford 2011*

You Are a Wave in the Ocean of God 2014

*365 Daily Prompts to Start the Day 2014
Spiritually Awake*

*Like a Cat Asleep On a Chair:
Advent Reflections 2016*

Haiku for Lent 2016

THE BIBLE EXPLAINED

BY EIGHT KISSES

E. Wayne McLaughlin

CreateSpace
4900 LaCross Road
North Charleston, SC 29406
USA

2018

Copyright © 2018 by E. Wayne McLaughlin

All rights reserved.

ISBN-13:
978-1985627604

ISBN-10:
1985627604

Published and printed on the CreateSpace platform. This book is available at Amazon.com and other online outlets.

Cover photo by Matthew Fassnacht on Unsplash

Dedicated to

my life partner

Patricia

whose kisses

are sweeter than wine

Table of Contents

INTRODUCTORY REMARKS 1

THE EROTIC KISS 3
    ROMANCE 3
    THE SONG OF SONGS 5
    LEVEL TWO: MYSTICAL LOVE 7
    LEVEL THREE: COVENANTAL LOVE 10
    MARRIAGE VOWS 11
    CARNAL INCARNATION 17
    THE RECAP 19

THE KISS OF BETRAYAL 20
    JACOB AND JUDAS 20
    DIS-ILLUSIONED 21
    THE PROBLEM OF EVIL 23
    THE PAINFUL TRUTH 26
    WITCH WAY? 27
    REVENGE IS SWEET 28
    WRITE TO RIGHT 29
    THE SAND AND THE STONE 30
    THE GIFT OF BETRAYAL 31
    BREATHE 32
    THE BREATH OF LIFE 35
    THE RECAP 37

THE KISS OF ACCEPTANCE 38
    SELF-ACCEPTANCE 39
    THE UNCONDITIONAL KISS 40
    THE GRAND INQUISITOR 41

THE SCANDAL OF GRACE	44
PAUL TILLICH'S SERMON	45
THE RECAP	46

KISSING IN CHURCH 48
THE KISS OF PEACE	49
THREE STEPS	51
THE OTHER EAR	52
THE HOLY HUG	52
THE HOLY CUDDLE	53
SYNCHRONIZED	54
CONNECTIONS	55
A DROP OF WINE	59
THE RECAP	61

THE KISS OF METAPHYSICS AND ETHICS 63
METAPHYSICAL TRUTH	63
THE SECOND BIG BANG	64
THE OPIATE OF UNBELIEF	66
SCIENTISM	67
INTERLUDE: THE EVOLUTION OF THE BIBLE	69
ETHICAL TRUTH	70
THE RECAP	75

THE GRATEFUL KISS 77
A SENSUAL SCENE	79
HOSPITALITY	79
FORGIVEN	80
THANKS	81
HEALTHY SUBMISSION	83
THE RECAP	88

THE KISS OF GRIEF 89
KISSES IN MILETUS	90

Tears	91
God, Grief, & Guts	93
Pepper in the Psalter	95
God's grief	97
Passionate God	103
The Recap	104
THE COSMIC KISS	**106**
Psalm 85	106
The Grammar of Salvation	108
Coming Together	110
Apocalyptic Nuptials	112
All shall be well	114
The Recap	116
EPILOGUE	**117**
NOTES	**118**

*May I print a kiss on your lips?' I said.
And she nodded her full permission;
So we went to press and I rather guess
We printed a full edition.*[i]

(Joseph Lilienthal)

Introductory Remarks

The word "kiss" in various forms is used 49 times in the Bible (56 if you count the Apocrypha). Genesis has the most kisses with ten. Luke has the most of the New Testament books with six. As I perused the references to kisses in Scripture I discovered that several of the "kissing verses" smacked of important themes in the Biblical narrative. On further reflection what became clear to me was that virtually the whole meaning of the Bible was represented in those sections of Scripture where human lips meet.

I don't claim to have covered every aspect of the Bible's message in the eight chapters of this book. But I believe you will find the essence of what the Bible and the Christian message are all about captured by the "kissing verses" covered in the following pages.

Writing from a Christian point of view, I hope to show that the Bible presents a vision of life that is holistic, inclusive, realistic, relevant, and challenging. My interpretation will vary from other Christians, of course. I come to the Bible from an ecumenical and humanistic perspective. The vision of life that I see in its story is one of liberation, healing, unity, and joy.

***

Abbreviations:

NRSV – New Revised Standard Version Bible, copyright © 1989 National Council of the Churches of Christ in the United States of America. Used by permission. All rights reserved.

[All quotations from the Bible are my own translation or paraphrase unless otherwise noted.]

BCE – before the common era. An interfaith equivalent of B.C.

CE – of the common era. An interfaith equivalent of A.D.

A note about language
I believe in inclusive language in reference to God and humans. The traditional use of the male pronoun for God has allowed a bit of idolatry to seep into the human unconsciousness. To view God in our minds as "he" is to set up a god who is literally male. The whole thrust of the Bible as well as official historical theology rejects a god made in the image of humans. The God revealed in the Jewish and Christian Scriptures is neither male nor female in a literal sense. The God we worship has neither gender nor a body. (Jesus said, "God is Spirit." – John 4.24.) Therefore, I have adopted gender-neutral language in reference to God. There are two problems with doing so. First, sentences sometimes do not flow as smoothly without pronouns. Second, the personal nature of God is not communicated as clearly without personal pronouns. It's a trade-off which I accept. The God of the Bible is personal in nature, but not a "person" as we think of human persons. God is love. And love is personal.

Chapter One

The Erotic Kiss

Romance

Let's begin with basics. When we think about kisses, we probably imagine romantic kisses. After all, without romantic kissing, you and I would not be here. The third chapter of the Bible brings up "nakedness," and sexual intercourse takes place in the fourth chapter. The Bible is not embarrassed by sex.

It says, "Adam knew Eve," and she conceived. Sexual intercourse is a deep knowing. And to know God is to have spiritual intercourse with God. Paul says in one of his letters,

> Don't you know that when a man has intercourse (κολλάω) with a prostitute he becomes one body with her? Remember how the Scripture says, *The two shall become one flesh*? In the same way, when you unite with (κολλάω) the Lord you become one spirit with the Lord (1 Corinthians 6.16-17).

The Bible is a book of romance. One of the most romantic passages in the Bible is when Jacob woos Rachel.

Jacob agreed to labor for seven years in order to marry Rachel, and time flew because he loved her so much (Genesis 29.20).

There is a lot of "he went into her" activity in the Holy Scriptures. I repeat: The Bible is not embarrassed about sex. It's basic. Men and women are chasing each other all through the pages of the Bible.

Yet, the human libido is only part of the romance. The greatest lover of Scripture is God. God is Israel's lover. The Holy One woos the Jews for centuries. They are sometimes faithful; at other times they are caught with their legs spread open for somebody else. But out of God's radical grace God will not give up on them.

God marries Israel: makes a covenant. In the New Testament there is a New Covenant and the Church becomes the Bride of Christ.

Please do not make the mistake of reading the Bible as a book of rules. It is a romance story. All of life is a romance—from the earthy level of humans being attracted to each other for procreation and pleasure, to the Creator offering Godself to all of us, to live in union and communion with the Divine.

The Song Of Songs

The most erotic book in the Bible is the Song of Songs (also known as The Song of Solomon). The Song begins with kisses.

> Kiss me on the mouth! For your kisses are sweeter than wine (1.2).

The Song of Songs can be understood on at least three levels. At face value it is a love story. Two people yearn for one another. They have erotic encounters. They speak or sing sensual words to each other. On this basic level the Song of Songs affirms the goodness of the erotic drive of our humanity and praises sexual arousal as the natural urge to be united with love. As one commentator on the Song of Songs writes: "Bouncing buttocks, phallic thrusts, heaving bodies, sighs and moans and giggles are all part of the God-given natural order of things."[2]

Because The Song was written so long ago and in a different place and culture, those of us in the West don't easily pick up on the erotic nature of the language. If you say to your wife or husband, "I'd like to climb your palm tree," they will not hear that as a romantic invitation unless they have become familiar with the terminology of The Song.

Here are some samples from The Song as rendered by the New Revised Standard Version:

(From Chapter four):

> You have ravished my heart...You have ravished my heart with a glance of your eyes...How sweet is your love...How

much better is your love than wine...Your lips distill nectar...honey and milk are under your tongue...

You are a garden locked...a fountain sealed...
Your channel is an orchard of pomegranates with all choicest fruits...a garden fountain, a well of living water, and flowing streams from Lebanon...

Awake, O north wind, and come, O south wind! Blow upon my garden that its fragrance may be wafted abroad. Let my beloved come to his garden, and eat its choicest fruits.

(From Chapter five):

I come to my garden. I gather my myrrh with my spice, I eat my honeycomb with my honey, I drink my wine with my milk.

(From Chapter seven):

How graceful are your feet in sandals...Your rounded thighs are like jewels...Your navel is a rounded bowl that never lacks mixed wine...Your two breasts are like two fawns, twins of a gazelle. Your neck is like an ivory tower.

How fair and pleasant you are, O loved one, delectable maiden! You are stately as a palm tree, and your breasts are like its clusters. I say I will climb the palm tree and lay hold of its branches. O may your breasts be like clusters of the vine, and the scent of your breath like apples, and your kisses like the best wine that goes down smoothly, gliding over lips and teeth.

> Come, my beloved, let us go forth into the fields… There I will give you my love. The mandrakes give forth fragrance, and over our doors are all choice fruits, new as well as old, which I have laid up for you, O my beloved.

The Song is a series of poems that use metaphors with deeper, juicier meanings than we see at first glance. At one level this Book of the Bible is definitely about lovers being aroused and making adventurous love.

Level Two: Mystical Love

On a second level this Biblical book expresses the soul's desire to connect with God and God's desire to be united with us. Song of Songs was the favorite Scriptural book of the Christian mystics. They used the strong erotic language to express the spiritual urge that our Creator has implanted within us.

Brother Wayne Teasdale, a Catholic monk, gives this summary:

> The Spanish mystics of the sixteenth century, Teresa of Avila and John of the Cross, conveyed their experience and its elaboration in terms of love-mysticism. They drew heavily on the bridal images of the Cistercians, notably Bernard of Clairvaux in the Twelfth century, developed insights from his own contemplative experience in the rich framework and symbolism of the Song of Songs… Both Teresa and John detail the stable mystical union known as the spiritual marriage—an unbreakable bond of profound affection in which the soul as the bride and God as the bridegroom, the lover and the beloved, become inseparable.[3]

Here is a quote from the 16th century mystic, St. Teresa of Avila:

> When He touches me I clutch the sky's sheets, the way other lovers do the earth's weave of clay. Any real ecstasy is a sign you are moving in the right direction, don't let any prude tell you otherwise.[4]

St. Teresa bears witness to her "orgasmic" encounters with Christ, her spiritual spouse.

St. Clair of Assisi (13th century), the friend of St. Francis of Assisi, expresses her relationship to Christ like this:

> Draw me after You! We will run in the fragrance of Your perfumes, O heavenly Spouse! I will run and not tire, until You bring me into the wine-cellar, until Your left hand is under my head and Your right hand will embrace me happily [and] You will kiss me with the happiest kiss of Your mouth.[5]

Again, this language is drawn from Song of Songs.

Marguerite Porete, a 13th century mystic, uses sexually charged terminology in her testimony of faith:

> I have said that I will love Him. I lie, for I am not. It is He alone who loves me: He is, and I am not...His is fullness, and by this I am impregnated. This is the divine seed and Loyal Love.[6]

As a result of her holy love-making, Marguerite has disappeared. Christ is everything. As St. Paul said, the ultimate goal is for God to be "all in all" (1 Corinthians 15.28). We shouldn't be surprised.

Kissing is the gateway gesture to intercourse. Marguerite says she is pregnant with God's love.

Though dozens of other examples could be shown, it is clear that the "kiss" at the beginning of Song of Songs smacks of mystical union with God/Christ. The mystics of the Christian faith (as well as the mystics of the other world religions) all speak of spirituality as intimate connection with God, as well as the sense of all things being interconnected. This view of reality is consistent with modern scientific knowledge. We live in a universe where Oneness is not a fantasy, but a reality. Spirituality and science converge at this insight.

Hildegard of Bingen, a 17th century mystic, says:

> As the Creator loves his creation, so Creation loves the Creator. Creation, of course, was fashioned to be adorned, to be showered, to be gifted with the love of the Creator. The entire world has been embraced by this kiss.[7]

Contemporary writer Paula D'Arcy tells us how physical romance and spiritual romance relate to each other:

> In the experience of romantic love, when many of the right elements seem to be present...I've often lived in the shadow of what is real, preferring the temporary "rush" of excited feelings to a pursuit of the truer Love that drives them. But the force *behind* the rush is what matters. It is the soul's longing to know itself, to find itself in life, and in that discovery to be aware of its relationship with all that is.[8]

Another contemporary spiritual writer, Father Matthew Fox, speaks about the mystical dimension of sexuality:

> [Sexuality] is important because for too long religion has moralized about sex. The real meaning of sexuality is deeply mystical. To make love is a theophany—a God experience. But the mystical dimension of sexuality has been missing in the West, even though we have a whole book in the Bible devoted to it, the Song of Songs, which celebrates lovemaking as an experience of the Divine…Nicholas of Cusa, the fifteenth-century mystic, said that every creature is a face of the one Face. So when you're face to face with another person, you're also face to face with the Divine.[9]

The 14th century Islamic mystic and poet Hafiz wrote:

> Anyone you have made love with, it is because you were really looking for God.[10]

Level Three: Covenantal Love

The third level of interpreting Song of Songs is accepted by Jewish and Christian scholars as the basic theological function of this brief book of the Bible. Jews read it as an analogy of the spousal relationship between God and Israel. Christians understand it to be speaking of the marital relationship between Christ and the Church. This husband-wife analogy is common in Scripture:

- In that day you will call God your husband (Hosea 2.16).
- God will marry you, Israel, and we will live happily ever after (Hosea 2.19).
- God will change your name to My Sweetheart; and your land will be called Matrimony (Isaiah 62.4).

- God said: I was Israel's husband, but she broke our marriage vows (Jeremiah 31.32).

Paul calls the Church the wife of Christ (Ephesians 5.22-23). In the Book of Revelation there is the portrayal of the wedding supper of the Lamb (Revelation 19.9).

Marriage Vows

I have found that one key to understanding the basic message of the Bible is the marital-analogy thread that runs throughout. I have identified twenty-five instances of what might be called *The Vow* in Scripture. (I'm sure I have missed one or more.) Its basic form is, "I am your God, and you are my people." There are variations of this statement.

Time and time again God makes this *Vow* to God's people—Israel and Church. God declares faithfulness to "his" spouse. (I quote the patriarchal language because in the Bible God is always presented as the Groom and God's people as the Bride. Today we may envision God as the Bride or the Partner.)

The important thing to see in this pattern is that the kiss of Song of Songs initiates and expresses a *loving relationship in which the two partners are bound to one another.* That is what the Bible is all about. Not doctrine or theology. Not concepts or ideas. But a relationship with the Divine. This relationship is characterized by commitment, faithfulness, loyalty, forgiveness, intimacy, and union. All three levels of interpretation include these characteristics.

I am presenting all twenty-five instances of *The Vow* at this point instead of placing them in a footnote or an appendix at the back of the book because I think the impact of seeing them all together might impress upon you how integral this marital language is to the Scriptural message.

Words in bold are the variations of *The Vow*. If the term 'covenant' occurs I will put it in italics as a reminder of the marital analogy.

Genesis 17.7-8
I will make a *covenant* between me and you and your descendants, an everlasting *covenant*, **to be your God**. I will give to you...the land...; and **I will be their God.**

Exodus 6.7
Then I will take you to **be my people, and I will be your God...**

Exodus 19.5
...if you will do as I say and keep my *covenant*, you shall **be my own possession** among all the peoples, for all the earth is mine.

Leviticus 26.12
I will be your companion and will **be your God,** and **you shall be my people.**

Deuteronomy 26.17-18
Today you have declared the Lord **to be your God**, and the Lord has today declared **you to be God's people, a treasured possession**, as God promised you.

Deuteronomy 29.13
You stand here today so that God may make you **God's people** and that God may **be your God**, just as God spoke to you and as God swore to your fathers, to Abraham, Isaac, and Jacob.

Jeremiah 7.23
This is what I said to them: If you obey my voice, **I will be your God, and you will be my people.**

Jeremiah 11.3-4
God said: Cursed is the person who does not take seriously the words of this *covenant* which I made with your forefathers when I brought them out of the land of Egypt, from the iron furnace, saying, Listen to my voice, and do what I tell you, and **you shall be my people, and I will be your God.**

Jeremiah 24.7 I will give them the desire to unite with me, for I am the Lord; and **they will be my people, and I will be their God**, for they will return to me with their whole heart.

Jeremiah 30.22 **You shall be my people, and I will be your God.**

Jeremiah 31.1 At that time, says the Lord, **I will be the God of all the families of Israel, and they shall be my people.**

Jeremiah 31.31-33 Listen, says God, the days are coming when I will make a *new covenant* with the people of the northern kingdom and the southern kingdom, but it will not be made of external laws like the one at Sinai. They broke that *covenant,* although I was a *husband to them*. But this new will be an internal one. I will put my law within them and write it on their heart; and **I will be their God, and they shall be my people.**

Jeremiah 32.37-40 I will bring them back to their land and they will be safe. **They shall be my people, and I will be their God...** I will make an *everlasting covenant* with them...

Ezekiel 11.19-20 And I will give them unity of heart, and place a new spirit within them. I will do an organ transplant by removing their heart of stone and replacing it with a healthy heart, so that they will be able to follow my instructions. Then **they will be my people, and I shall be their God.**

Ezekiel 14.10-11 When the prophets give false messages and the people believe them, I will discipline all of them so that they may learn to stay on the right path. Thus **they will be my people, and I shall be their God**, declares the Lord God.

Ezekiel 34. 25, 30-31 I will make a *covenant of peace* with them....Then they will know I am the Lord **their God**, and that I am present with them, and that they **are my people,** declares the Lord God. As for you, **my sheep**, the sheep of my pasture, you are mortals, and **I am your God,** declares the Lord God.

Ezekiel 36. 25-28 Then I will sprinkle clean water on you, and you will be cleansed of your dirty idolatry. Moreover, I will give you a new heart and insert a new spirit within you; and I will remove the heart of stone from your chest give you a heart of softness. I will put my Spirit within you and cause you to follow my instructions. You will live in the land that I gave to your forefathers; so **you will be my people, and I will be your God.**

Ezekiel 37. 23, 26-27 I will liberate them from their old sinful haunts and wash them clean. And **they will be my people, and I will be their God.** I will make a *covenant of peace* with them; it will be an *everlasting covenant*. And I will give them a safe place where they can populate the land. They will have a place of worship and my home shall be in their midst. **I will be their God, and they will be my people.**

Hosea 2.23 I will also have compassion on her who had not been shown compassion, and I will say to those who were not my people, **"You are my people!"** And they will say, **"You are my God!"**

Zechariah 8.8 ...and I will bring them back to live in Jerusalem; and **they shall be my people, and I will be their God** with faithfulness and justice.

Zechariah 13.9 And I will test the third that survive, just as silver is purified and gold is tested in the fire. They will call on my name, and I will answer them, saying, **"You are my people,"** and they will say, **"The Lord is my God."**

[This form of the *Vow* that follows, from John's Gospel, is not usually perceived as a covenantal statement, but it is, in my opinion. The first half of the vow/promise is not spoken; rather it is enacted by the resurrection of Christ. By resurrecting Christ, God is in effect saying to the Church, "See, I have been faithful to my vow. I have not left you or divorced you. I'm still here. Death could not break our bond. I have brought Christ back to you, even through death." In other words, **I am still your God.** Then Thomas pronounces his part of the vows: **Yes, you are still 'my Lord and my God.' I belong to you.** Most commentators assume that Thomas is calling Christ "God." But I think Thomas is speaking his part of the marriage covenant: You are mine. And I am yours. It's not necessarily a statement about Christ's divinity. It is certainly a statement about covenant faithfulness—belonging to one another, and keeping the promise.]

John 20.27-28
Then the Risen Lord said to Thomas, "Put your finger in my side." Thomas replied, **"My Lord and my God!"**

2 Corinthians 6.16 Or what agreement has the temple of God with idols? For we are the temple of the living God; just as God said, "I will make my home among them and live among them; **and I will be their God, and they shall be my people."**

Hebrews 8.8-10 Behold the days are coming, says the Lord, when I will create a new *covenant* with the Jewish community...I will write my instructions internally—right into their hearts and minds. **And I will be their God. And they shall be my people.**

Rev. 21.3 And I heard a loud voice from the throne, saying "Look! God's home is in the midst of the people. **They shall be God's people,** and God will be among them **and be their God.**

I hope it is now clear that "I will be your God, and you will be my people" is a major them throughout the Bible—a theme that frames the marital/spousal relationship that is central to the Bible's story. It would not be an over-simplification to say that the whole purpose of the Bible is to alert us to the fact that God is wooing us for marriage. God is seeking us. God wants an intimate relationship with each of us individually and collectively.

Go on the internet or to YouTube and search for "nuns marry Jesus," or "monks marry Jesus." You will find videos and articles that describe or show the ceremony that Christian monks and nuns go through as they take their vows and enter the monastery as full members. The ceremony is a wedding ceremony. They marry Christ.

But this relationship is not just for nuns and monks. Every Christian at baptism takes vows and enters into a Covenant with Christ. We are all "married" to Christ; and the Church collectively is the Bride of Christ.

The Bible is a proposal. All God wants is for us to say Yes, then live that Yes every day.

Carnal Incarnation

There is something strange about Song of Songs. *God is absent.* Well, at least God is not mentioned anywhere in this brief book. (Only one other book in the Bible shares this strange phenomenon, the book of Esther.) But I would affirm God's presence in the Song even though God is not named.

Wherever love is, there God is. Whether it is the carnal love between two human beings or the mystical love between the Spirit and a person, God is present. God is hidden beneath the sheets of love, in the prayers of faith, and in the acts of kindness and compassion. Whenever you forgive someone, God kisses you.

The kiss that begins Song of Songs invites us into a sensual spirituality and a religion that is drunk with love. God is our Lover. We have spiritual intercourse with God. The Bible is about union. God is not a distant, abstract Intelligence. God is our partner, our intimate companion.

Christians refer to Jesus as the *in-carnation* of God because Jesus was a bodily being. He was the Word of God en-fleshed. Jesus was a real human being, not a disguise. He wasn't wearing a Halloween costume, pretending to be a real human being. He was really flesh (human).

Saint Bernard of Clairvaux gave eighty-six sermons from Song of Songs and only got part way through the book. The first sermon was given during Advent and was based on the first two verses. Bernard took the line, "Let him kiss me with the kisses of his mouth," and applied it to the meaning of Christmas. He wrote, "The mouth that kisses signifies the Word who assumes human nature." So, the mouth which God uses to kiss us is God's Word made flesh in Jesus of Nazareth. By means of Jesus, God kisses us—makes contact.[11]

The kiss of Song of Songs reveals not only our relationship with others and our relationship with God, but also God's relationship with Godself. The early church writers saw deep theological significance in the "kissing verse." They found the whole Trinity there.

Let him kiss me refers to God the Father; it is the Father who does the kissing. The *mouth* is God the Son who speaks God's Word and becomes God's incarnate Word. The *kiss* itself is God the Holy Spirit who unites the Father and the Son, and unites the Son with us.[12] Wow! Don't tell me theologians cannot be creative. The whole Trinity in one smooch! Yet, today's Christian theologians tend to emphasize the *relational* nature of the doctrine of the Trinity. The terms *father and son* speak not of gender, but of relationship. The Holy Trinity is about the holiness of relationships as modeled in the inner essence of God.

The Recap

The kiss of Song of Songs shows us that the Bible is about God's *romance* with us. The Bible is not a book of rules or a book of religious ideas. It is a love story.

The Bible…
- affirms the sensual, sexual, physical, and material realities of life
- reveals that the "urge to merge" is the primary drive in life, expressed sexually and spiritually
- values relationships above all else
- shows the mystical impulse that drives us toward connection
- agrees with the modern scientific view that everything is interconnected
- tells the story of divine-human union, using the metaphor of marriage

Chapter Two

The Kiss of Betrayal

Jacob and Judas

The very first kiss in the Bible is a kiss of betrayal. Jacob deceives his father by pretending to be the older son, Esau. (His father, Isaac, was losing his sight.) When Isaac asks his father for a kiss, Jacob kisses him. It is a deceptive kiss.

> Then Isaac said to Jacob, "Come here and kiss me, my son." So he came near and kissed him. Isaac smelled the clothes Jacob wore; they smelled like the clothes Esau would wear. So, Isaac gave the blessing to Jacob and said, "Ah, the smell of my son is like the smell of a field that the Lord has blessed" (Genesis 27:26-27).

We all know who betrayed Jesus. But do you remember the kiss? The scene is the Garden of Gethsemane. Jesus is praying and struggling with fear. He asks God to "take away the cup" of suffering from him. After much prayer, Jesus commits himself to "drink the cup" and become the sacrifice that will shake the world.

> Jesus was still talking to Peter, James, and John when another disciple—Judas Iscariot—arrived. Judas had with him a large crowd that had been gathered by the chief priests and the elders of the people. They were carrying swords and clubs. Now the betrayer had given them a sign, saying, "I

will kiss the man you want. When I kiss him, arrest him." At once he came up to Jesus and said, "Greetings, Rabbi!" and kissed him. Jesus said to his betrayer, "Friend, do what you have to do." Then they came and grabbed Jesus and arrested him (Matthew 26:47-50).

Dis-illusioned

People will let you down. You will let yourself down. The Biblical message is not naïve. It is not for no reason that Jesus teaches us to pray, "Deliver us from evil." Evil exists. Not in the form of a red devil with a long tail and a pitch fork. There is no real person called Satan, just as there is no real person named Uncle Sam. But we know Uncle Sam exists in the feelings and loyalties of the citizens of the United States. And we know that the Devil/Satan exists in the behavior of people and systems that resist goodness and justice and peace.

The German theologian Dietrich Bonhoeffer warned against a naïve type of Christian faith when he wrote his book, *Life Together*:

> Innumerable times a whole Christian community has broken down because it had sprung from a wish dream. The serious Christian, set down for the first time in a Christian community, is likely to bring with him [or her] a very definite idea of what Christian life together should be and try to realise (sic) it. But God's grace speedily shatters such dreams. Just as surely as God desires to lead us to a knowledge of genuine Christian fellowship, so surely must we be overwhelmed by a great general disillusionment with others, with Christians in general, and, if we are fortunate,

with ourselves. By sheer grace God will not permit us to live even for a brief period in a dream world.[13]

It is easy to become irritated by the behavior of our family members or fellow workers or strangers. But it shouldn't be so in the church. The church should be a place where people are kind and loving and forgiving; a place where people get along. Well, let me tell you—having been a church professional for forty years, I have no illusion about the church. I've met some of the meanest, back-stabbing people in the church. The dark side of human nature is not completely erased at the moment of baptism or joining the church. "Conversion" is a life-time project. Even in the church, people will betray you.

One of my favorite verses in the Gospels is in Matthew where Jesus tells his disciples, *Be as shrewd (φρόνιμος) as snakes and as innocent as doves (10.16).*

Carl Sandburg reminds us of the animalistic dimension of human nature:

> *There is a wolf in me . . . fangs pointed for tearing gashes . . . a red tongue for raw meat . . . and the hot lapping of blood—I keep this wolf because the wilderness gave it to me and the wilderness will not let it go.*[14]

The Bible uses quaint language for this human situation: sin, wickedness, transgression, iniquity. Modern evolutionary biology uses other terminology: instinct, mismatch, inherited proclivities, reptilian brain, DNA, genetics, limbic system, natural selection.

Whether one uses biological terminology, poetic metaphors, or mythic language, the reality of destructive, inhuman, or self-defeating behavior is all around us and within us. The *kiss of betrayal* is part of the realism of the Biblical message. In fact, one of the main criticisms of the Bible is that it is full of violence. It is most definitely an R-rated book.

Part of the function of the Biblical narrative is to hold up a mirror so we can see what we are like, warts and all. The Sacred Book pulls no punches. People can be vicious.

I like the realism of Paul when he says to the Christians in Rome, *Be at peace with everyone, if at all possible (Romans 12.18).* Sometimes it is not possible.

The Problem of Evil

The age old question is "Why?" Why is there betrayal or any other kind of evil in our world? There are various attempts to answer this difficult question.

Hobbes said that we have "a perpetual and restless desire of power after power, that ceases only in death."[15] Rousseau disagreed. He said that we are basically good people, but society and its institutions corrupt us.[16] Darwinians say that natural selection and the struggle for survival make us genetically inclined toward violence and selfishness.[17]

There is a Jewish legend that says when God consulted with the angels about whether or not to create human beings the angels of mercy and righteousness said, "Let them be created because they will do merciful and righteous deeds." But the angels of peace and truth said, "No. Do not create them. They will be full of falsehood and will quarrel all the time." God thought about it for a while and decided to go ahead and create the humans. According to the story,

God believed that humans would become better and less destructive over time. In secular terms that is what the Harvard neuroscientist Steven Pinker argues in *The Better Angels of Our Nature*.[18]

Professor of World Religions, Huston Smith, tells us that secular philosophies and other rational systems of thought cannot deal with the "problem of evil." They always come to a dead end. But religious thought has another resource, called variously, the third eye, the eye of the soul, the eye of the heart, or simply "vision." He asserts that intuitive vision gives an answer to the problem of evil:

> If a two-year-old drops her ice cream cone, it's the end of the world for her. The question is, Can there be a vision of reality—not just a reality we see, but an all-encompassing reality—that places even the worst evils we can imagine, like the Holocaust or a huge plague, in the position of a dropped ice cream cone in the context of the total infinite perfection of things?[19]

In other words, religious faith can intuit a Larger Reality that transcends time. And from the perspective of that Reality much of what we experience as evil or painful or absurd or tragic will be understood in a different way, and be seen as part of a larger redemptive drama. Theologically this is referred to as *eschatology*.

For people with a purely secular point of view, this approach to understanding evil may seem like a cop-out or a dismissal of the tragic, or even a mean-spirited way to talk in the context of human pain and suffering.

A mature Christian perspective agrees with the last objection. It is not an appropriate or loving thing to offer an "other-worldly" consolation to suffering people in many cases. The loving thing to do is to *be present to* those who are suffering or reacting to tragedy.

That is no time to try and provide answers or solve theological riddles. To take a person's pain or suffering seriously we have to be in the moment with them—sharing their pain without explanation. The exception might be for a religious believer who is experiencing tragedy, yet finds comfort in the vision of the Larger Picture.

But in a neutral context of discussion regarding the problem of evil, the Biblical message offers a vision of reality that transcends our limited access to time and place. The Bible does not give a cogently logical answer to the reality of evil. But it does assert that evil is not the *kiss of death* in an ultimate sense. There is more to reality than meets the eye.

Some folks will ridicule the Biblical vision as just so much "pie in the sky by and by" nonsense. But in a literal sense, it *is* non-sense: it is a truth claim beyond our *sense* perception. The only alternative vision is to grit one's teeth in the face of the meaningless and cruel absurdity of life. Camus has his followers. But I am not one of them. You can pretend to "make meaning" if you want to. But invented meaning is not real Meaning to me. It is counterfeit.

Like Martin Luther I'll have to say, *Here I take my stand.* Life does have meaning in spite of the unexplainable evil and suffering in it. The meaning is real and *given*. And it is a meaning that has its roots in eternity. Such a belief does not distract me from concern for our present earthly problems, whether they be ecological or political or psychological. We are here on this good earth to enjoy its blessings and work on the continuing creative project of our Creator. Because I live and work for justice and peace out of a context of eternal meaning, I do not despair at temporary defeat; nor do I feel compelled to adopt the so-called winning strategies of Machiavellian deception or violence. Survival has its place, but integrity (righteousness) has a higher place in the order of the moral universe. Otherwise, it is dog-eat-dog.

Yet I give the last word to contemporary theologian Bernard Sesboüé: "When we wonder about evil, we actually do not know what we are asking. For we seek to understand something that is incomprehensible. Evil is the irrational par excellence, something irretrievable, something that reason really cannot make sense of... Our reflection on evil can only be modest, and it always leaves much to be desired."[20]

The Painful Truth

There are no shadows without light. The presence of light is what makes shadows possible. In a similar way, the hurt that comes from betrayal would not be possible if love did not exist. The great Christian thinker C.S. Lewis said:

> To love at all is to be vulnerable.
> Love anything and your heart
> will certainly be wrung and possibly be broken.
> If you want to make sure of keeping it intact,
> you must give your heart to no one…[21]

We cannot avoid pain in this world. Simon and Garfunkel sang "I am a rock, and a rock feels no pain." If we try to live life without getting hurt, we end up stone cold. The moment we choose to be part of the great divine Movement of Love in the world, we have signed up for some kind of pain.

We have a choice. We can choose our pain. But we cannot choose to live in this world without any pain. Our choice is either the pain that comes with loving and being loved; or the pain of isolation and loneliness. If we choose love we become vulnerable to betrayal, grief, and emotional hurt. But it's worth it. Life without love is more painful still. (Note: when I speak of life with love, I'm not implying the necessity of marriage. Single people can also give and receive love in a variety of ways.)

Witch Way?

In January of 1692 some teenage girls in Salem Town, Massachusetts began acting strangely. They made weird movements, twitching and jerking, and claiming that some invisible force was poking and pinching them. They were finally pressured into identifying the tormentor. They blamed Tituba, the Parrises' Caribbean slave, and two eccentric social outcasts, Sarah Good and Sarah Osborne.

Hysteria broke out as other girls began experiencing similar phenomena. The authorities began rounding up dozens of people, accusing them of witchcraft, and putting them in jail. Governor William Phipps ordered the formation of the special Court to examine the situation.

On June 10 Bridget Bishop was hanged as a witch. She was the first of nineteen executions. A 20th victim, Giles Cory, was tortured to death when he refused to enter a plea. In October, Governor Phipps abruptly dissolved the Court and prohibited further arrests. (It may have been because some girls had accused the Governor's wife of witchcraft.) Over an eight-month period, more than 200 people had been accused and imprisoned, and several had died in jail.

Some of the judges and examiners later expressed remorse. Examiner John Hale wrote in 1695, "Such was the darkness of the day, and so great the lamentations of the afflicted, that we walked in the clouds and could not see our way."[22]

Where does evil come from? Sometimes it is the result of the darkness of ignorance, the clouds of chaos, or the fog of fear. While suffocating on the cross Jesus asked God to forgive his tormentors because, he said, "They know not what they do." Ignorance is dangerous. Many New Testament scholars argue that Judas turned Jesus into the authorities, hoping to force him to react and initiate a violent revolution against the Roman occupiers. A misunderstanding or a lack of education can easily lead to tragedy. The *kiss of betrayal* represents the Bible's recognition of the ongoing need for education and enlightenment.

Revenge is Sweet

The real question is this: when we receive the kiss of betrayal, how will be respond? Perhaps our natural instinct is to "get back" at our betrayer. Some people think that the meaning of justice is: *you hit me, so I will hit you back.* But such an idea has nothing to do with what our Scriptures call "justice." Hitting back is vengeance.

We see the desire for vengeance all through the Bible, maybe most often in the Psalms. David says:

> Lord, my good friend, the one I trusted, who stopped by often for dinner, has kicked me while I'm down. He has betrayed me! Lord, please have mercy on me and make me well again so that I can get up and pay them back! (Psalm 41:9-10)

At least it's an honest prayer. We would all do well to be so frank with God. But it hurts, doesn't it? It's one thing to be betrayed by someone who is not close to us; but it's another thing to be stabbed in the back by a close friend or family member. "How dare you!" we say. "You can't trust anyone!" It is natural to feel burning rage within. What we do at that point depends on how mature we are.

Write to Right

It may take some time to work through our anger. We can't keep it to ourselves. It is wise to write down (or type) our thoughts and feelings regularly for several days. One strategy is to write our betrayer a letter, or a series of letters (or emails), but never send them. Writing something down is a powerful action. Novelist Anne Tyler said (in a different context), "For me, writing something down is the only road out." Putting our feelings down on paper has a liberating effect.

Or consider an "anger journal." Mahatma Gandhi's grandson, Arun Gandhi, said he learned from his grandfather how to recognize his own anger, which is the beginning of nonviolence—realizing you are angry and knowing the reason why. He said, "Grandfather taught me to write an anger journal, to write down my feelings whenever I was angry. Instead of putting the anger toward another person or thing, I poured it out into the journal to find a solution."[23]

In addition to writing, talking is a healing activity. Go to a trusted friend or counselor and tell your story of betrayal. Speaking thoughts and feeling out loud is another powerful strategy in dealing with our pain.

Write. Talk. Repeat again and again.

Eventually, if we have taken time to tend to our broken heart, we will be able to move forward in a positive way.

The kiss of betrayal shocks us into reality. Even though human beings are good by nature (see the first chapter of Genesis where God pronounces everything created "good"), we frequently allow our essential goodness to be blocked or covered up. Our destructive behavior does not reveal who we are; instead, it shows what happens when pure water becomes contaminated.

Many unseen factors are at the root of our unloving and malignant words and actions: genes, upbringing, illness, psychological complexes, corrupting experiences, what we put into our bodies, images we feed upon from the screen, a lack of emotional intelligence, brain disease, social forces, etc. We are complex beings, and there is never just one thing going on.

The Bible is no Pollyannaish book. It is full of violence and hatred and bigotry. It tells of life the way it is. There is injustice in life; and there is betrayal. Get used to it! The important question is: how will we respond?

The Sand and the Stone

A story tells of two friends walking through the desert. During some point of the journey they have an argument, and one friend slaps the other in the face. The one receiving the slap bends down and writes in the sand: *Today my best friend slapped me in the face.*

They keep walking until they find an oasis where they decide to take a bath. The one who had been slapped gets stuck in the mire and begins to drown, but his friend intervenes and saves him. After he recovers from the near drowning, he writes on a stone: *Today my best friend saved my life.*

His friend asks him, "After I hurt you, you wrote in the sand, but now you write on a stone. Why?" The other says, "When someone hurts you, you should write it down in sand where the winds of forgiveness can erase it. But when someone does something good for you, you must engrave it in stone where no wind can ever erase it."[24]

A simple story, but a profound lesson. Each of us must decide which experiences of our lives will be preserved in our emotional center and which ones we will allow to be blown away by the strong winds of forgiveness. Jesus tells us that the Spirit of God is like the wind (see John 3), and I suppose we can imagine the Spirit shifting the sands of time in order to bring healing to one who has been hurt.

The Gift of Betrayal

It was the philosopher Friedrich Nietzsche who said, "That which does not kill us makes us stronger."[25] The *kiss of betrayal* is a horrific experience, and I don't mean to speak about it lightly. The pain is real, and healing is an arduous journey. Nevertheless, the message of the Bible resonates with many other ancient traditions, as well as modern psychological insights, when it leads us to learn from our painful experiences.

Lucie Johnson, Obl.S.B., has written a brave and wise prayer that expresses such a response to betrayal:

[…]
Before those who have hurt me
    and harmed me,
those who have made my life difficult,
those who have betrayed me,
those who hated and despised me,
those of whom I was afraid,
I bow in gratitude.
Their challenges have stretched me.
I have learned much
    about dark places within.
In time, compassion has taken root
    within me,
my heart has grown larger,
able to love and hold more.
Their gift seemed very bitter,
    but it was precious too.
Bless them, Lord,
and may the compassion they have fostered
envelop them also
and mend all their broken places.
Amen.[26]

Breathe

The act of exhaling literally produces a small wind. The Bible also speaks of the Spirit of God as the "breath of God." Jesus breathes on the apostles and gives them authority to forgive sins (see John 20). The very act of breathing, if done with spiritual intent, can be a form of prayer.

In Christian history the teachers of contemplation say that paying attention to our breathing can work as a method of prayer. For example, the fourth century monk, Macarius, said, "Say with each breath, 'Our Lord Jesus, have mercy on me.'" The monk Hesychios wrote, "Let us live every moment in 'applying our hearts to wisdom' (Psalm 90.12), as the Psalmist says, continually breathing Jesus Christ, the power of God the Father and the wisdom of God (1 Corinthians 1.24)."

In the 14th century St. Gregory Palamas gave this instruction: "That is why some teachers recommend to the beginner to pay attention to the exhalation and inhalation of their breath, and to restrain it a little, so that while they are watching it the intellect too may be held in check."

Nicephorus the Solitary, a monk of Mount Athos in Greece, wrote, "And so, having collected your mind with you, lead it into the channel of breathing through which air reaches the heart and together with this inhaled air, force your mind to descend into the heart and to remain there."[27]

But how does focusing on breath help us deal with betrayal or other negative experiences? This is where interfaith relationships enable us to expand our skills for spiritual living.

Many Christians have found that the Buddhist method of prayer called Tonglen can be adapted as Christian prayer.

The Dalai Lama explains the purpose of Tonglen as…

> …the Mahayana practice of "giving and taking." When one undergoes the experience of pain and suffering one thinks, "May my suffering substitute for all similar types of

suffering that sentient beings may have to undergo."...So in this way one takes others' suffering upon oneself.[28]

The method is simple. As you inhale, you take into your heart the suffering and evil of the world (or a particular person). As you exhale, you breathe out peace to the world (or to a specific person). Praying like this for ten or twenty minutes purifies your heart and sends the power of grace throughout the world. It can change you too. Here is the description of this method of prayer as described by the sisters of the Visitation Monastery of Minneapolis:

> Tonglen meditation is one tool we draw on to teach the transformation of struggle and suffering. In this Buddhist meditation practice, we find the intersecting Christian teachings of compassion and forgiveness and the Salesian virtue of gentleness. In the process of this practice, we may experience deep consolation and healing. We invite you to try it.
>
> Here are the abbreviated steps of this meditation practice. Find a comfortable posture, palms up, eyes closed, feet on the ground. This work takes great courage. Trust your ability to do it, as you align with your heart's deepest wells of love and the mercy and kindness you possess.
>
> 1) Identify a source of suffering or struggle within your own life. How have you experienced hurt? Fear? Resistance? Doubt? Shame? Breathe in the experience, imagining it as hot, heavy air or smoke, including the feelings that accompany your hurt. Let them touch every part of your being. Exhale loving kindness and mercy. Imagine this as light, loving air.

2) Consider the suffering or hurt of a beloved friend or family member. Breathe in their pain, recognizing you are not alone in your struggle. See how they hurt in their circumstances and invite the mercy and kindness of your heart to transform this woe. Exhale loving kindness.

3) Recognize the hurt or pain in an acquaintance – someone you see on the street, driving in a car, in your place of work, or at the gym or grocery store. Breathe in their pain, and exhale loving kindness.

4) See your would-be enemy, and envision how they hurt. Let their struggle enter your imagination, and trust your heart's ability to be softened and hold their pain. Inhale deeply and exhale loving kindness and mercy.

5) Consider your pain, that of your beloved, what ails the acquaintance or stranger, and that of your would-be enemy as one: inhale the collective hurt of all and exhale loving-kindness. Recognize how connected all suffering is, and your power to send love and light, joy and kindness to all.[29]

The Breath of Life

One way to visualize what the death of Jesus means is to imagine God inhaling all the evil of the world through God's "mouth" (Jesus), and exhaling peace and grace back into the world through God's "mouth" (Jesus)—the breath itself being the Holy Spirit. As a thought experiment, this visualization presents the Trinitarian movement of the Sacred within history that has brought "fresh air" to the human experiment in our little corner of the universe.

The Bible is not the story of some mythic Zeus on Mount Olympus who never touches the ground. Rather, the Jewish-Christian Scriptures narrate the tale of living, breathing, down-to-earth people in specific geographical locales. For Christians, the historical figure of Jesus reveals what happened to a specific individual in the Middle East in the first century, and what meaning his life and death has for humanity.

Jesus of Nazareth was executed like thousands of other Jews were, by crucifixion. Crucifixion was a method of asphyxiation. Having one's arms stretched out with the body hanging down makes it extremely difficult to breathe. After a period of time the victims do not have the strength to lift their body up to take in a breath. Jesus was killed by cutting off his breath. But before taking his last breath he said, "Abba, forgive my betrayers. They do not understand how evil their actions are." Then, "he breathed his last."

The Bible is the story of the Source of life. In the beginning poem in Genesis one, the Source "breathed into the creature the breath of life, and it became a living soul." This same Source has been part of the air we breathe all through human history. At one point in human evolution the Source inhabited a Jewish man in a unique, defining way, so that through that person the Breath of life walked among us and showed us that Ultimate Reality is the power of love.

The story of the resurrection of Christ shows us that the Breath of life cannot be smothered. The story of Pentecost (Acts 2) tells of the Breath coming as a "mighty wind," initiating a movement of reconciliation: divisions are destroyed; barriers are broken down; races, religions, nationalities, social classes, and genders are unified under the power of Love.

As the Source gives mouth-to-mouth resuscitation to the human race, it may appear to be a kiss. Perhaps it is.

The Recap

The kiss of betrayal found in Scripture reminds us that life is difficult; that we shouldn't expect everything to go our way, nor be surprised when good people do bad things.

The Bible…
- warns us against living a naïve life
- is realistic about evil in the world
- promises us a rose garden—one with lots of thorns
- does not see evil and suffering as an intellectual stumbling block for faith, but simply as a fact of life
- offers a positive response to pain inflicted by others—the way of forgiveness
- gives wise counsel about healthy responses to evil
- tells the story of Jesus whose selfless response to betrayal places the Cross in history as the symbol of transformation and healing
- teaches us that responding in healthy ways to the darkness around us is part of becoming a mature person

Chapter Three

The Kiss of Acceptance

It is one of the best known stories in the New Testament. There is a family—a father and two sons (see Luke 15). Both sons work on the family farm. But one day the younger son decides he is bored with farm work. He knows that he will inherit some money when his father dies. "But why wait?" he tells himself. So he approaches his father and asks for his share of the inheritance. We are not told about this conversation. I wonder if the father objected. Did he sit down and try to reason with his son? And why did he allow this young man to pre-empt the normal procedure? Perhaps his permission reflects the fact that God our Father allows us to make choices, take risks, and fall on our face.

You know the story. The son goes off into a far country. Perhaps present-day Turkey or Iran or Afghanistan or Spain. We don't know.

Far away from home, the son wastes his money. (The word *prodigal* means to waste or be extravagant. Here it refers to the son's activities, but later it may refer to the father's mercy.) With all his money gone, he has to find a job. All he can find is the one job no self-respecting Jew would do: feed pigs. (Jews didn't eat pork. Pigs were considered "unclean" animals.) But a man's got to do what a man's got to do. He works for minimum wage and can't pay his bills. And he gets very depressed.

Self-Acceptance

Finally he "comes to himself" (Lk. 15.17). Now that's an odd phrase. It implies that he has left himself. Perhaps it relates to our phrase, "He was beside himself." Can you picture that? Can you picture a person standing beside another person that is her doppelganger? What's going on? Has she been cloned? If I go out of myself and have to come back to myself ("he came to himself"), it implies that I have been split apart. My "I" and my "self" are divided. It means self-alienation or self-estrangement.

It is as if this young man had pushed himself outside himself. And by rejecting his own self he is left with an empty husk of a self. His self's "house" is vacant. No one home. Foreclosure.

So many of our personal problems and so many societal problems are caused by the lack of self-acceptance. When we loathe ourselves, we end up loathing others too. The daily news is filled with headlines about violent acts. Perhaps ninety percent of the violence we read about originates within a foreclosed self. When a house is empty for a long time and begins to deteriorate it eventually is condemned. In like manner a person who lacks self-acceptance eventually feels herself to be condemned.

The great spiritual writer Thomas Merton had been a monk at the monastery near Bardstown, Kentucky for seventeen years when he wrote in his journal on October 2, 1958:

> Finally I am coming to the conclusion that my highest ambition is to be what I already am. That I will never fulfill my obligation to surpass myself unless I first accept myself... Original sin was the effort to surpass oneself by being "like

God"—i.e., unlike oneself. But our Godlikeness begins at home. We must first become like ourselves and stop living "beside ourselves."[30]

The Prodigal Son takes the first step toward self-acceptance. He resolves to go back home. But he still doesn't quite get it. He believes that the best result he can realistically expect is to work for his father as a servant.

The Unconditional Kiss

What a surprise. One would expect the father to greet his son with sarcasm: *So, you come crawling back home, huh? You wouldn't listen to your old man, but now here you are, slouching back to daddy. You got what you wanted. Don't think you can come back here as if nothing has happened. You are going to pay for what you've done!* That response was what the young man was expecting. He had his speech ready. *I am not worthy to be called your son. Please, just let me work as a hired hand.*

But Jesus says,

> *While the young man was still a long way off, his father squinted his eyes and saw that it was his son coming down the road, and he was deeply moved with love and jumped up and ran as fast as an old man could run, and hugged his son with a big bear hug and kissed his dirty face and washed it with his tears* (Luke 15.20).

The father kissed his son with the kiss of unconditional love! The parent accepted the child without any strings attached. There was no

"If…then." There was just love, period. This is what the Bible calls "grace." As Paul put it,

> *We have been saved by grace, not by what we have accomplished or anything else* (Ephesians 2.8).

The self-acceptance that had begun to blossom within the son now came to full bloom in the sunshine of divine acceptance. You know the rest of the story: The son received a robe, a ring, and new shoes. Then the father threw a party. There was singing and dancing and eating and drinking and lots of hugging.

And you know that the older son refused to go to the party. He was too much of a law-and-order guy. He believed that if you didn't follow the old rule of "an eye for an eye" and give immoral people what they deserved, the whole social order would collapse.

Of course it was more personal than that. The older, more responsible son, was jealous. He worked hard for his dad because he thought it was the condition for being accepted and loved. But now he saw that all of his work was for naught, at least in *his* mind. Somehow the elder son had based his life and effort on the doctrine of *conditional* love. This *unconditional* love shown by his father made him mad. It tore down his whole system of morality and his sense of self-worth built on accomplishment and moral decency.

The Grand Inquisitor

Perhaps the most significant kiss found in literature is in Dostoyevsky's great novel *The Brothers Karamazov*. One of the Karamazov brothers (Ivan) has written a fictional story. He calls it "The Grand Inquisitor." He tells the story to his brother Alyosha.

It is set in Spain in the sixteenth century. Christ surreptitiously comes back to earth and walks the streets of the Spanish town and heals people. Crowds gather around him. A powerful Cardinal of the Church shows up with guards and arrests Christ. Late that evening the Cardinal visits Christ in his cell to explain why he has been arrested.

The Cardinal (known as the Grand Inquisitor) tells Christ that his actions are detrimental to the Church. He reminds Christ of the three temptations offered him by the devil in the wilderness and how his refusal to give in to the devil had guaranteed free will for all human beings. According to the Grand Inquisitor free will is too heavy a burden for humanity to bear. It is dangerous to allow people to choose to follow Christ's teachings and fail; and thereby end up damned forever.

What Christ should have done, says the Cardinal, was to give no choice; rather, he should have taken control of everyone's choices so no mistakes would be made—and the people could live in securely.

The cardinal explains to Christ that the Church has corrected his error by taking away the free choice of people and replacing it with security. That's why Christ must be kept in prison and away from the people, so that he is not tempted to give freedom back to the people.

He further explains that the Church had to take over power from the Roman Empire and allow Satan to do his job in order to bring happiness to the people.

The tale ends likes this:

> When the Inquisitor fell silent, he waited some time for his prisoner to reply. His silence weighed on him. He had seen how the captive listened to him all the while intently and calmly, looking him straight in the eye, and apparently not wishing to contradict anything. The old man would have liked him to say something, even something bitter, terrible. But suddenly he approaches the old man in silence and gently kisses him on his bloodless, ninety-year-old lips. That is the answer. The old man shudders. Something stirs at the corners of his mouth; he walks to the door, opens it, and says to him: "Go and do not come again…do not come at all…never, never!" And he lets him out into the dark squares of the city. The prisoner goes away.[31]

The only response Christ makes to the inhumane proposal of the Grand Inquisitor was a kiss. It was an act of love and mercy. Radical mercy. The Inquisitor could not response with any kind of rational argument. His heart was so touched by the kiss that he became merciful and let the prisoner go. Once you have been kissed by Christ you cannot be the same again.

God's response to human hatred or human indifference is a kiss. Golgotha marks the spot where the Creator kissed us. Christ's response to his betrayers, those who abandoned him, those who beat him during interrogation, the religious leaders and the government that put him to death was a response of unconditional love, grace, and self-emptying.

The Scandal of Grace

But this is part of the scandalous meaning of the Bible's message. Traditional religion has sometimes warped into the "Older Son" mindset. It has preached a moralistic message that rewards bourgeois respectability and condemns anyone who gets out of line. Jesus himself was criticized by practitioners of such moralistic religiosity.

(Be clear that I am not saying Jesus was a victim of "the Jews" or Judaism. Jesus himself was a religious Jew. In the first century Judaism was having intra-Jewish debates over how to be faithful to the LORD. All major religions have these debates within their own families of faith, including Christianity.)

Jesus tells the story of the Prodigal Son as a way of stressing the extravagant love of the Prodigal Father. Some would call it wasted love. But God has so much love to share that it is never wasted; it is an ever-flowing stream. As the Psalmist says, *The mercy of the Lord is from everlasting to everlasting* (Psalm 103.17).

To me personally, the kiss in Luke 15 is the most precious of the Biblical kisses. I have struggled with a lack of self-acceptance all my life. In those moments or days when I truly accept and love myself, it is because of the kind of God revealed to me by the core message of the Bible. I keep putting conditions on myself, but the grace of God does an intervention and brings me back to my senses; i.e., grace helps me "come to myself" – my real self.

Paul Tillich's Sermon

The best extra-Biblical presentation of the meaning of grace I know of is a sermon given by the German theologian Paul Tillich. Here is a portion of that sermon:

> Do we know what it means to be struck by grace? It does *not* mean that we suddenly believe that God exists, or that Jesus is the Saviour (sic), or that the Bible contains the truth. To believe that something *is,* is almost contrary to the meaning of grace. Furthermore, grace does not mean simply that we are making progress in our moral self-control, in our fight against special faults, and in our relationships to [other people] and to society. Moral progress may be a fruit of grace; but it is not grace itself, and it can even prevent us from receiving grace...
>
> Grace strikes us when we are in great pain and restlessness. It strikes us when we walk through the dark valley of a meaningless and empty life. It strikes us when we feel that our separation is deeper than usual, because we have violated another life, a life which we loved, or from which we were estranged. It strikes us when our disgust for our own being, our indifference, our weakness, our hostility, and our lack of direction and composure have become intolerable to us. It strikes us when, year after year, the longed-for perfection of life does not appear, when the old compulsions reign within us as they have for decades, when despair destroys all joy and courage.
>
> Sometimes at that moment a wave of light breaks into our darkness, and it is as though a voice were saying: "You are accepted. *You are accepted,* accepted by that which is greater than you, and the name of which you do not know.

Do not ask for the name now; perhaps you will find it later. Do not try to do anything now; perhaps later you will do much. Do not seek for anything; do not perform anything; do not intend anything. *Simply accept the fact that you are accepted!"* If that happens to us, we experience grace.

After such an experience we may not be better than before, and we may not believe more than before. But everything is transformed. In that moment, grace conquers sin, and reconciliation bridges the gulf of estrangement. And nothing is demanded of this experience, no religious or moral or intellectual or presupposition, nothing but *acceptance.*[32]

In less theological language, the Presbyterian minister known as Mr. Rogers, told children the same thing: *I like you just the way you are.*[33]

The Recap

The core message of the Bible tells us that God is not out to condemn us. Rather, God accepts us as we are and works with us to keep maturing. There is nothing we have to do, nothing to earn. We are invited to accept the fact that we are accepted. The Bible's message is one of grace which is symbolized by the father's kiss on the face of his son.

The Bible…
- uses the metaphor of a forgiving parent to tell us that God is forgiving, with no strings attached
- overcomes the image of an angry, wrathful God in its presentation of the Good News proclaimed and embodied in Jesus

- invites each of us to accept ourselves unconditionally
- teaches the radical and scandalous life style of unconditional love toward each other
- critiques moralistic styles of religion as a distortion of the Good News of the deep reality of God's grace
- has a message which can set us free from self-loathing

Chapter Four

Kissing in Church

No one knows how it happened. The man was on an international flight. He went into the restroom and flushed himself down the toilet and out the plane into the ocean. He miraculously survived and began to swim until he came to a small island. He soon discovered that he was the only one on the island. Six months later a small plane flew over and spotted him. A rescue team was sent. He was so happy to see them. He had lost weight, yet survived. The team noticed that he had built three huts. They asked the man about them. "Oh," he said, pointing, "that one is my house. That one over there is my church. And that other one is my former church."

Unfortunately, many churches are like the cells in our body: they grow by splitting. Life is prone to divisions. Racial bigotry. Divorce. Nationalism. Sectarianism. Party politics. Personal inner alienation. Why is there so much division?

As part of the evolutionary process, *homo sapiens* have developed a tribal mentality for the sake of survival. As soon as we identify as a member of a particular tribe, we create an "us" and a "them." Tribalism in its modern form of nationalism with its racist components has set human beings against one another. Greeks saw non-Greeks as barbarians. Germans called Jews vermin, lice, a cancer in the body of the nation. In Rwanda, Hutus called Tutsis cockroaches. In the American South, whites treated Blacks as sub-human.

The narrative of the Bible tells of our tribal existence and the consequences of our group identity. Much of the violence found in the Bible (some of which is attributed to God's command) is a portrayal of our evolutionary stage of development in which we huddle together for safety. Yet, the core message of the Bible works counter to the tribal mentality.

Thirty-six times the command to love the stranger appears in the Torah (first five books of the Bible).

> *You must not mistreat or oppress the stranger in any way. Remember, you yourselves were once strangers in the land of Egypt (Exodus 22.21).*
>
> *You must not oppress strangers. You know what it feels like to be a stranger, for you yourselves were once strangers in the land of Egypt (Exodus 23.9).*[34]

The Kiss of Peace

The majority of Christian churches all over the world do something during worship called *Passing the Peace*. It is a brief period when people greet each other with words such as, "The peace of Christ be with you." They may shake hands or hug or kiss. This practice goes all the way back to the beginning of Christianity. It is mentioned five times in the New Testament.

- Aquila and Priscilla, along with the church that meets in their house, send warm greetings to you in the Lord. In fact, all the believes here send their greetings. Greet one another with a holy kiss (1 Corinthians 16.19-20).

- Say hello to one another with a holy kiss (2 Corinthians 13.12).

- Greet each other with a sacred kiss (Romans 16.16).

- Greet all of our sisters and brothers in Christ with a holy kiss (1 Thessalonians 5.26).

- Greet one another with the kiss of love (1 Peter 5.14).

The usual place in the liturgy for the Passing of the Peace is just before the Offering and Communion. This reflects the words of Jesus in the Sermon on the Mount:

> So when you are bringing your gift to the altar and suddenly remember that someone has something against you, just leave your gift in front of the altar, and go—find that person and make things right between you. Then go back to worship and place your gift on the altar (Matthew 5.23-24).

This is what congregants do ritually in churches every Sunday around the world. They shake hands or hug or kiss, to show that they are at peace with one another.

Three Steps

A few chapters after the Sermon on the Mount, Jesus suggests a procedure for making peace. This is from Matthew 18:

1. Jesus says: If someone does something to hurt you, it is your responsibility to go to that person and talk about. Don't go public with it or tell anyone else. Just the two of you should work it out in private. If the two of you can make peace and be reconciled, then you have won a victory.

2. But if he or she will not cooperate, find one or two other good people and go back and try again.

3. If the other will still not cooperate and work with you toward a solution, the next step is to make it a family affair. Bring to bear the influence of the family of faith.

And it's at the end of this passage that Jesus says,

> Whenever two or three of you come together in my name [to make peace], I am there with you.

The unseen partner in our movements toward reconciliation is Christ.

It has been my experience that the Church in its many institutional forms has incorporated the "Matthew 18 peacemaking structure" into its official rules of discipline. An orderly, judicial system is in place that comes straight from the Bible.

The Other Ear

There's a story that comes from early Methodist history in American. When the circuit riding preacher came to town, a female member of the church asked for a home visit. The preacher went to the woman's home and listened as she complained about another member of the church. As she told her story the preacher stuck a finger in one of his ears. This distracted the woman enough that she paused her story and asked him why he was doing such a thing. He said, "Oh, I'm just keeping this one ear for the other side of the story."

Because we all perceive events from our own perspective, there is never just one story. Therefore, we are obliged to listen to each other to get the whole picture. It's like putting together a large jigsaw puzzle with someone else. We don't have all the pieces. We need the other person's pieces too.

The Wisdom Tradition of the Bible gives good advice along this line.

- Always be willing to listen and slow to speak (James 1.19).
- If you give an answer before listening to what someone else has to say, you act in a stupid manner (Proverbs 18.13).

The Holy Hug

A priest told about the time a about a parishioner came to ask for guidance. It was close to Thanksgiving Day, and the man was concerned about the annual visit with his wife's family. "Every year I end up fighting with my mother-in-law," he said. The priest told him to pick a saint, one he thought might be able to help, and to pray to that saint every night, asking for help.

A few days after Thanksgiving the man reported to the priest about his experience over the holiday. "I want to thank you," he said. "I followed your advice. I chose Saint Francis. I prayed every night. I told him: *Francis, you hung around with some pretty undesirable people, so I think you can understand my problem. Please help me with my mother-in-law.* And guess what! This is what Francis told me: *I once hugged a leper, and if I could do that, you surely can hug your mother-in-law.*"

And that's what the man did. When Thanksgiving Day came, the first thing the man did was to give his mother-in-law a warm hug. "She was so surprised she started to cry," he told his priest. "And we had a great day."[35]

Why was it a great day? Because the son-in-law did what the Sermon on the Mount advises. He took the initiative. He sprang a surprise on an unsuspecting family member. He used the *Holy Hug* strategy. Surprise can be an effective way of rearranging the conflictual situation in some cases.

The Holy Cuddle

In New York City men and women are paying to be cuddled. They pay $80 an hour to cuddle with a stranger. Now don't jump to conclusions. I know it sounds shady. But there are rules. The professional "cuddler" will not allow anything inappropriate to take place. It is purely Platonic cuddling. People are so hungry for affection that they will pay for it. These are people with no families or people who don't have time for close relationships. The service of non-sexual cuddling nourishes their humanity.[36]

It reminds me of men and women in nursing homes or similar facilities who say they yearn to be touched. Some have said that they feel like "untouchables" because visitors keep their distance as if old age is contagious.

Jesus certainly had a ministry of touch. He put his hands on the heads of children and blessed them. He reached out and touched blind eyes and withered hands. People were healed and restored to fellowship with others. Here is an example:

> There was a man with leprosy who knelt in front of Jesus and said, "Lord, if you want to, you can heal me." Jesus reached out and touched the man's body and said, "You are healed." And indeed, the man's leprosy disappeared (Matthew 8.1-3).

A Holy Touch is kin to the Holy Kiss. It is a gesture of love and peace. Appropriate, non-sexual touching can close the gap of alienation and bring peace to the lonely, the self-loathing, and those in need of affection. Let me stress that context matters and that physical and psychological boundary issues must be observed. Just as the holy kiss within a liturgical setting follows specific guidelines, a loving touch in the proper setting can be a peaceful action.

Synchronized

A recent study had twenty-two couples who had been together at least a year to hold hands while undergoing brain scans. The women either sat holding hands with their partners, sat nearby but did not touch them, or were in a different room. The scenarios were then repeated, but this time the women were subjected to mild pain.

Overall, the women found that holding hands reduced the intensity of their pain by an average of 34%. The brain scans showed that when the couples held hands their brain waves synchronized, and that this 'coupling' effect was even greater when the women were in pain. The researchers speculate that supportive touch could help people feel understood, which may trigger pain-reducing reward systems in the brain.[37]

What Christians do in worship when they "pass the peace" is ritual practice for real life. The *kiss of peace* was/is an actual touching event. When two people consent to touch each other with loving intent, *that* is a powerful action. Personal distance is overcome. Peace and harmony are activated at an epidermal level. Skin to skin mending takes place. We not only speak words of peace, we feel peace being transmitted through our nerve endings.

Not only personal pain, but social and ecological pain needs our tender touch. The world is out of sync. The Christian understanding of our calling as human beings is one of working towards reconciliation, facilitating the synchronization of our lives—creating harmony between all people.

Connections

In Hungary there is an ultra-nationalist political party called the Movement For a Better Hungary which goes by the name "Jobbik." It has been described as fascist, neo-Nazi, racist, and anti-Semitic. It has accused Jews of being part of a "cabal of Western economic interests" attempting to control the world. Until 2012, one of the party's leading members was a politician in his late twenties named Csanad Szegedi. But some of Jobbik's members wanted to stop his influence in the party. They began to research his background. They found that his maternal grandmother was a Jewish survivor of Auschwitz. So was his maternal grandfather, and half of Szegedi's family was killed during the Holocaust. Szegedi did not know about his ancestral history. But as the rumors began to spread, he did his own research and found that the rumors were true.

After Auschwitz, his grandparents, once Orthodox Jews, decided to hide their identity. When his mother was 14, her father told her of the secret and ordered her not to reveal it to anyone. As Szegedi found the truth about himself he decided to resign from the party and find out more about Judaism. He went to a local rabbi, Slomo Koves, who at first thought he was joking. Nonetheless he arranged for Szegedi to attend classes on Judaism and go to the synagogue.

At first, Szegedi says, people were shocked. He was treated by some as a "leper." But he persisted. Today he attends synagogue, keeps Sabbath, and has learned Hebrew. In 2013, he underwent circumcision.

As the realization that he was a Jew began to change his life, it also transformed his understanding of the world. Today he says his focus as a politician is to defend human rights for everyone.[38]

The solution to our divisive tribalism is to discover that our identity is much larger than any tribe can contain. When Christians *pass the peace* to one another they are expressing a larger truth about themselves and all of humanity. The Biblical message tells us that there is only one race—the human race. All divisions are artificial. That's not to say that ethnic and cultural differences are not real. Rather, as each ethnic or cultural group shares its unique gifts with the larger family of humanity, the differences blend to create a more interesting community.

The Church finds its identity "in Christ." It's not meant to be an exclusive club. To be "in Christ" is to recognize that we all come from the same transcendent Source, that all people are connected and related as one Family, and that we are meant to live in peace with one another.

You do not have to be a Christian to live "in Christ." Our identity is a meta-identity. The New Testament word *repent* literally means to *expand your thinking.*

> Greek term for repentance is *metanoia.*
> *Noia* means "mind."
> *Meta* means "beyond."
> *Metanoia* indicates a mind that goes beyond;
> or expanding our small mind into the Larger Mind
> (of God);
> or going beyond our small way of thinking as we
> commit ourselves to more inclusive way of thinking
> that is embodied in Christ's ministry.

To repent is to move from the narrow mind to the Wide Mind of the God who loves the whole world. *(For God so loved the world...)*

St. Paul told the Roman Christians to be *transformed by the renewal your mind (Romans 12.2).*

Our divisions are healed as we overcome our small way of thinking by broadening the boundaries to include all. We are reconciled to God and to one another as we enter an *inclusive identity.* The *we-them* feelings give way to the *us-feeling.* The fear and hostility that split us apart are overcome by the kind of love revealed in the Christ-story—the type of love that unites us in our common humanity.

The *kiss of peace* puts us in touch with the original oneness that our Creator intends for our world.

The Christian claim that *God was in Christ reconciling the world to Godself (2 Corinthians 5.19)* is in the Christian mind a universal claim. The Bible calls Christians to work for the reconciliation of all people.

In the New Testament Letter to the Ephesians, the writer says that in the execution of Christ the wall that divides races has been broken down (see Eph. 2.13-18). Jews and non-Jews have been united to create a New Humanity.

The *kiss of peace* is a visible sign of the New Humanity created by Christ. It is also a call to work against the tribal tendencies that are part of our evolutionary heritage. To unite our lives with Christ is to experience a spiritual mutation in our evolutionary journey.

This is hard work. It goes against the grain of the human inclination to risk one's safety. Those who criticize Biblical religion, saying it offers an infantile consolation, have not yet understood the core message of the Bible which calls for mature, brave, and risky response to the angry divisions of humanity.

The Christian invitation to be "in Christ" is an offer of finding one's ultimate identity not in a national creed or a race or an ideology, but in our common humanity as children of God. The Bible's core message is a *spiritual humanism* rooted in transcendent reality. The *kiss of peace* therefore may be understood as an affirmation of our full humanity. It is not a call for everyone to adopt a Christian Creed; rather, it is an expression of an Ultimate Love that unites the whole universe and entices earthlings to embrace one another as one family.

A Drop of Wine

The Dalai Lama and Archbishop Tutu have developed a friendship. In 2015 the two religious leaders met at the Dalai Lama's home in Dharamsala, India to spend some time together and share their religious traditions.

On one morning the Dalai Lama talked about his practice of meditation, and they meditated together. Then it was the Archbishop's turn to share a tradition. He and his daughter Mpho got the communion bread and wine ready. The Dalai Lama said, "A Buddhist monk does not take wine or any alcohol—in principle, that is. But today, with you, I will take a little. Don't worry, you can rest assured, I will not be drunk."

It is unusual for an Anglican and a Buddhist to worship together. In fact, even among Christians there is not universal agreement about sharing Holy Communion. During my pastoral career I served an ecumenically yoked parish in southern Indiana. I was the pastor of a small Presbyterian Church (PCUSA) and a Lutheran Church (ELCA) in the same small town. Those two congregations had no problem celebrating the Sacrament of Communion together. There was another Lutheran Church in the same small town. But it was a different kind of Lutheran Church—a Missouri Synod Lutheran Church. The irony was that while the two churches I served could have Communion together the Missouri Lutheran Church would not allow members of the Evangelical Lutheran Church to receive the Sacrament there.

But the Archbishop and the Dalai Lama broke with convention. Mpho and her father handed out the small prayer booklets, and the service began. The Dalai Lama nodded his head attentively. When they stood he wrapped his crimson cloak around him, his hands pressed together, his fingers laced.

Mpho Tutu wore a bright red dress and a matching red headscarf. She began with a prayer for all of those places where injustice exists, where there is strife, and continued to offer prayers of healing for all of those who are in need. The words, "Peace be with you," were spoken, and everyone went around to kiss and embrace one another. The Archbishop and the Dalai Lama held hands and bowed to each other.

Now was the time for Communion. The Archbishop lifted up a small piece of Tibetan white bread and placed it in the Dalai Lama's mouth. One could see the beaded UBUNTU bracelet on the Archbishop's wrist. *Ubuntu* is an African word that affirms the connectedness and interdependence of one another.

Then Mpho approached with the glass of red wine. The Dalai Lama dipped the tip of his left ring finger into the glass and placed the smallest drop into his mouth. The service ended as Archbishop Tutu said, "Go in peace to love and serve the Lord. Hallelujah. Hallelujah."[39]

The Church's *kiss of peace* is a tangible expression of God's desire that all the barriers to human friendship be broken down. The Archbishop's willingness to serve the Sacrament to a Buddhist, and the Dalai Lama's willingness to dip his finger in the wine, is a small illustration of what the Bible is about. The human traditions that keep us apart can be overcome when we are led by the Spirit. The Transcendent Reality that motivates Buddhists to live compassionately is the same Reality that motivates Christians to love their enemies; and the same Reality that moves atheist scientists to search for the truth, and energizes social movements for freedom and equality.

The *kiss of peace* is the kiss of reconciliation, unity, and solidarity. The core message of the Bible is about the moral imperative that people come together, that the gap of hostility or suspicion be closed, and that the organic unity of Nature be appreciated and guarded.

The *kiss of peace* is not mouth-to-mouth resuscitation; it is mouth-to-mouth reconciliation. *God was in Christ reconciling the world to Godself (2nd Corinthians 5.19)*. Make no mistake about it—any person or force which intentionally divides or deceives or creates fear is not aligned with the Biblical Narrative.

The Recap

The Bible is about unity. Through mythic as well as historical narrative the Christian Scriptures realistically report the brokenness of our world and show the path to wholeness. The entire Biblical message could be summarized as the movement from Union to Disunion to Reunion.

The Bible…

- recognizes that division is a part of the human story

- reveals that God's intention for the world is unity

- tells of the early Church's creation of a ritualized practice during worship which expresses God's intention

- tells of the Church's ordered process for conflict management

- recognizes the healing potential of touch

- states that God (in Christ) has acted to reconcile the world and overcome division

- calls us to work for global friendship

- invites all people to realize their identity in the one Human Family

Chapter Five

The Kiss of Metaphysics and Ethics

> Proverbs 24.26:
> One who gives an honest answer
> gives a kiss on the lips. (NRSV)

To be honest is to tell the truth. And truth is certainly one of the themes of the Bible. The reality of Truth points in two directions: the metaphysical and the ethical.

Metaphysical Truth

The 18th and 19th century Enlightenment movement decided that Metaphysical Truth was out the window along with religion and faith. The new Truth was scientific Truth. If it can't be tested and proved by the scientific method, then it can't be called True. A belief in non-scientific Truth is mere superstition. Any belief in non-material (spiritual, religious, faith-based, philosophical) facts is only in one's imagination. If it is beyond the physical realm (i.e., of the meta-physical realm) and can't be put to the scientific test, it is irrelevant and fictional. In the 20th century this approach to Truth was known as "positivism."

Is there something "beyond the physical"? The first theologian, St. Paul, wrote:

> But, as the Hebrew Scriptures say: "There are some things that can't be seen with our eyes, nor heard with our ears, nor known by our imagination—things God has prepared for people who love God," – and these realities have been made known to us through the Spirit. All reality is researched and proven by the Spirit, even the Divine Abyss. We humans can't even understand ourselves unless we go down into the unconscious. It's the same way with metaphysical Truth: It takes the non-material Being of Spirit to truly comprehend the non-physical realities of God's creation—realities that are not subject to scientific proof. (1 Corinthians 1.9-11, my colloquial paraphrase)

Later to the folks in that same city, Paul wrote:

> We look not at what can be seen but at the invisible reality. What we can see is temporary—subject to the laws of science, but spiritual reality is not subject to the scientific method; the spiritual is not boxed in by the limitations of human knowledge. (2 Corinthians 4.18, my anachronistic paraphrase)

Simply put, the *kiss of honesty* points to the Bible's assertion that there are unseen realities which cannot be detected through the microscope or telescope.

The Second Big Bang

A prime example of the Biblical assertion of Metaphysical Truth is the resurrection of Christ. According to our present day worldview, the resurrection of the body is impossible because it is outside any understood and accepted scientific framework. Dead people do not come back to life!

There are two problems with such a statement. First, Christ did not *come back* to life. That would be resuscitation, not resurrection. The report of the New Testament is that Christ *went forward* into a new kind of life—a *new creation.*

This points to the second problem. Our objection to the possibility of a resurrected body is part of our present framework, what Christian theology would call the *old creation.* The resurrection of Christ doesn't fit into the *old creation;* it is precisely the revealing of a *new creation.*

St. Paul says,

> All of you who have entered the reality of Christ have become part of a New Creation [καινὴ κτίσις]. The Old is gone, the New has come for you (2 Corinthians 5.17).

This new creation is mentioned again in Paul's letter to the Galatians:

> All of this controversy about whether or not one is circumcised really doesn't matter. What really matters is being part of God's New Creation [καινὴ κτίσις] (Galatians 6.15).

What the New Testament asserts is there has been a *second Big Bang,* initiated by the resurrection of Christ.

The resurrection of Christ is part of a new framework of existence that has partly arrived in human history and partly still in the future.

Our present scientific understanding of the world is not equipped to capture the new framework with its present technology. Christ gives us a glimpse into the future New Order through his resurrection into a new kind of bodily existence in which a body can materialize and dematerialize. When we read the Gospels' accounts of his appearances this is what we see: a new kind of body, not a resuscitated body.

So, the present day disbelief in Christ's resurrection based on our present understanding of existence doesn't take into account the possibility that God (who is the Creator) has already initiated a New Existence in Christ. Likewise, the objection which says that the resurrection could not have taken place because only those events which are repeatable can be tested misses the point that the resurrection of Christ was a one-time event (until the final resurrection). If we insist that God can work only in our little Box, then we have shut ourselves off from the larger reality of divine possibilities.

This brings me back to the beginning of this discussion. Metaphysical Truth (or spiritual reality) cannot be dismissed because we can't grasp it. We limit our knowledge if we superstitiously believe in only that which we can see.

The *kiss of honesty* invites us to keep an open mind about the possibility of unseen realities that the Biblical message speaks of.

The Opiate of Unbelief

Eastern Orthodox theologian David Bentley Hart reminds us of a common logical mistake often made by spokespeople for science:

> While a given method may grant one a glimpse of truths that would remain otherwise obscure, that method is not itself a truth…Quite a few otherwise intelligent men and women take it as an established principle that we can know as true only what can be verified by empirical methods of experimentation and observation. This is, for one thing, a notoriously self-refuting claim, inasmuch as it cannot itself be demonstrated to be true by an application of empirical method.[40]

The claim that there is only one way to know what is real—the scientific method—is an assertion without proof. World Religions professor Huston Smith said that in order for science qua science to recognize the existence of God it would have "to admit there is an intelligence greater than ours, and since the tool kit of science can't get its screwdrivers into that, it means that they don't have the whole story."[41]

When a scientist says, "But there is no evidence of God," we need to remember Stephen Jay Gould's aphorism: "Absence of evidence isn't evidence of absence."

Materialism—the belief that there is nothing beyond material reality—is for some people a comfortable philosophy—what Czeslaw Milosz liked to call "the opiate of unbelief."[42]

Scientism

Ian Hutchinson is Professor of Nuclear Science and Engineering at MIT, where his research group explores the confinement of plasmas hotter than the sun's center, aimed at producing practical energy from nuclear fusion reactions, the energy source of the stars. In his book, *Monopolizing Knowledge,* Hutchinson differentiates "science" from "scientism." He says, "Scientism is the belief that all valid knowledge is science. Scientism...assumes that rational knowledge is scientific, and everything else that claims the status of knowledge is just superstition, irrationality, emotion, or nonsense."[43]

One of the common ways modern proponents of atheism talk about reality is by reducing everything to the smallest parts. They remind us that when it gets down to the most basic elements reality, there is nothing but atoms and molecules. That's all there is. Donald Mackay in his book *The Clockwork Image* coined the term "nothing-buttery" to refer to such reductionism. He writes, "Nothing-buttery is characterized by the notion that by reducing any phenomenon to its components you not only explain it, but *explain it away.*"[44]

Ian Hutchinson comments on this type of reductionism this way:

> So yes, I am an assembly of electrons and quarks interacting through quantum chromodynamics and the electroweak forces; yes, I am a heterogeneous mixture of chemical elements predominantly hydrogen, oxygen, and carbon and their compounds; yes, I am a wonderful system of biochemical processes guided by genetic codes; yes, I am a vast and astoundingly complex organization of cooperating cells; yes, I am a mammal, with hair and warm blood; yes I am a person, husband, lover, father; ...I am all of these things and not one of them is less true than any other. In no case is it correct to say I am *nothing but* one of these descriptions. Not one of these descriptions necessarily rules out the others, once we set scientism aside.[45]

An analogy which may be helpful for the sake of visualization is given by the Biblical professor John Walton. He invites us to think about a layer cake. The bottom layer is the realm of scientific observation, investigation, and explanation. The top layer represents the work of God—the science of theology. The two disciplines of theology and science do not compete because they exist at different layers or levels. The bottom layer might be identified as the layer of secondary natural causation while the top layer is identified as ultimate causation. Science, by current definition, cannot explore the top layer. Both layers are part of the same reality.[46]

Scientism denies that there is a "top layer." The Biblical narrative tells the story of how human history has been fed from the top. The top and the bottom do not contradict each other.

The danger of scientism is its tendency toward "nothing-buttery." When we do not recognize that the whole is more than the sum of its parts we reduce humans to mere atoms and molecules—the result being a dehumanizing approach to life. Authentic science does not dehumanize. It is only when science becomes an ideology (scientism) that it over-steps its bounds and begins to behave like a religion.

The *kiss of honesty* points us toward the Biblical sense of reality and keeps us honest about who and what we are and the limitations of our intellectual disciplines.

Interlude: The Evolution of the Bible

Science and the Bible share a parallel process. Both evolve. As new information comes to light, scientific knowledge changes. By continual experimentation and examination of evidence, scientists reinterpret older discoveries and update our understanding of reality.

A similar process takes place in the realm of spirituality. As scholars discover additional ancient documents, our understanding of Biblical language, culture, and religious practice is updated. As theologians dialogue with current culture and with theological traditions, they suggest new ways of conceptualizing religious truth. Our understanding of God evolves as our human consciousness evolves. We refine our idea of God as we experience the world in new ways.

Both the scientific discipline and the discipline of theology live by hypotheses that are provisional and open to change. John Henry Newman wrote the famous *Essay on the Development of Christian Doctrine* (1845) to show how even many dogmas cannot be dogmatically held. God does not change, but our human conceptualization of God does.

Just as science has progressed from Newtonian physics to quantum mechanics, theology has moved from Augustinian and Thomistic systems to Process Theology, Liberation Theology, Queer Theology, and so on. Our lived experience opens our eyes and minds to broader and deeper perspectives. The Biblical Narrative evolves in this way.

Ethical Truth

Now let us move beyond the discussion of metaphysical truth to the area of human behavior. To be truthful is to be ethical and moral.

As I've said earlier in this book, the Bible is not a rule book. It doesn't give us an absolute list of dos and don'ts. Of course there are commandments and prohibitions and admonitions all over the

Bible. But there is no presentation of a systematic ethical code for all people in all times and places.

Much of what we find in the Bible that has to do with what is right or wrong is situational. Some commandments apply to people long ago, but not to people today. Many statements that say, "Don't do this," are limited to a particular historical or cultural context.

For instance, Leviticus 19.19 says, *You shall not put on a garment made of two different materials.* But none of us think that is a commandment for us today (except for some strict Jewish sects). In 1 Timothy 2.12 we read: *No woman may teach or have authority over a man.* Church and society (in large part) have moved beyond the first century belief in the inferiority of women.

A key phrase to remember when interpreting the Bible is: *That was then. This is now.*

When it comes to ethics, the Bible's concern is not about keeping rules or obeying commandments; it is about what kind of person we are and how we relate to others.

Jesus summed it up when asked about what really mattered. He said: *There are two commandments that you should follow: Love God with your whole being. And love others as much as you love yourself. Everything hangs on these two principles (Matthew 22.36-40).* We should note that his answer is chosen from his Jewish Bible (Deuteronomy 6.5 and Leviticus 19.18).

The rest of the New Testament agrees. From Paul's letters:

To the Romans…

> Owe no one anything, except to love one another; for the one who loves another has fulfilled the law. The commandments, "You shall not commit adultery; You shall not murder; You shall not steal; You shall not covet"; and any other commandment, are *summed up* in this word, "Love your neighbor as yourself." Love does no wrong to a neighbor; therefore, love is the fulfilling of the law (Romans 13.8-10, NRSV).

To the Galatians…

> For you were called to freedom, brothers and sisters; only do not use your freedom as an opportunity for self-indulgence, but through love become [servants] to one another. For the whole law is *summed up* in a single commandment, "You shall love your neighbor as yourself" (Galatians 5.13-14, NRSV).

To the Corinthians…

> If I speak in the tongues of mortals and of angels, but do not have love, I am a noisy gong or a clanging cymbal. And if I have prophetic powers, and understand all mysteries and all knowledge, and if I have all faith, so as to remove mountains, but do not have love, I am nothing. If I give away all my possessions, and if I hand over my body so that I may boast, but do not have love, I gain nothing… And now faith, hope, and love abide, these three; and the *greatest of these is love* (from 1 Corinthians 13, NRSV).

Love as the foundation for ethics is rooted in the nature of God.

God is love (1 John 4.16).

We can't get any more basic than this. The whole Biblical Story is about Love. For Christians, basic reality is Love. Love is not just a characteristic of God or an attribute of God, it is God's essence. Therefore, Biblical ethics is grounded in love. Love as "defined" by Jesus.

What is love? Look at Jesus. Read the gospels. Watch him. Listen to him. He is Love embodied. Love incarnate.

The *kiss of honesty* in an ethical sense comes down to this: Relate to others in a Christ-like manner.

Of course, to live ethically is not a simple matter. I don't want to over-simplify. Life is ambiguous; therefore, ethical and moral decisions are full of ambiguity. But the guiding principle we receive from the Bible is love. Christ-like love.

Even as love carries within itself the dynamism of expansion, our application of the love-ethic also expands to include the whole of nature. Nature is also our "neighbor." Ecological realities and environmental concerns come under the umbrella of love's parameters. Christian love is not just for individuals, but for the whole organic system. And in relation to political, economic, and social systems, love expresses itself as justice and equality. The prophetic tradition of the Bible focuses on the need to help the poor, the marginalized, and the powerless. Both personal and systemic causes and solutions come into play in the Bible's approach to ethics.

We are responsible for deciding what "love" calls for in each situation. Instead of being guided by a rule book we are to be guided by the Spirit:

> Live by the Spirit... If you are led by the Spirit, you are not subject to the law [Torah]...The fruit of the Spirit is love, joy, peace, patience, kindness, generosity, faithfulness, gentleness, and self-control. There is no law against such things... If we live by the Spirit, let us also be guided by the Spirit (from Galatians 5, NRSV).

The New Testament uses various phrases synonymously:

- to be led by the Spirit
- to be guided by the Spirit
- to be led by the Spirit of Christ
- to have the mind of Christ
- to follow Jesus

Pope John Paul II wrote that "Christian morality consists in the simplicity of its Gospel: that of following Jesus Christ, of abandoning ourselves to Him, and of letting ourselves be transformed by His grace and renewed by His mercy." The Pope goes on to speak about the important role of conscience.

> Conscience is the most secret core and sanctuary of a person, where we are alone with God. In the depths of our conscience, we detect the moral law, which does not impose itself upon us, but which holds us to a higher obedience. This law is not an external human law, but the voice of God, calling us to free ourselves from the grip of evil desires and sin, and stimulating us to seek what is good and true in life.[47]

St. Augustine sums up Christian ethics this way: *Ama et fac quod vis – Love and do whatever you want.*[48]

The Recap

I've taken the liberty to use a small verse from Proverbs to point to the larger matter of Truth: metaphysical truth and ethical truth. The Bible is a narrative about the Truth. It doesn't deny that there are relative truths. But it assumes the existence on an Absolute Truth. That one Eternal Truth is God. The Biblical Story does not present a philosophical argument. Rather, it tells a story.

The Bible...

- asserts that reality is bigger and deeper than what one can see with one's eye

- bears witness to the resurrection of Christ from the dead, not as resuscitation, but as a new kind of body/reality never before seen

- says that the 'Christ Event' (his life, death, and resurrection) was the beginning of a New Creation

- presents a vision of life that is completely compatible with modern science

- recognizes different ways of knowing, the scientific method being one way, but not the only one

- dignifies humanity by describing *homo sapiens* as 'the image of God'

- rejects any reductionist approach to reality which would take away respect for the inherent dignity of humanity

- points to the Wholeness of reality that cannot be reduced to its parts

- gives us a flexible approach to moral and ethical decision-making

- contains commandments, prohibitions, and rules that no longer apply

- says that the ethical life is summed up in the commandment to love God and others—extending to the whole creation

- undergirds our modern ecological sensitivity with its dogma of the goodness of creation/nature

- 'defines' love through the way Jesus lived and related to people

- asserts that the essence of God is love

- says we are free to live joyful lives as we are led by the Spirit, with no need to be obsessed with rules and laws

- teaches that we have an inner sense of the moral life residing in our conscience

Chapter Six

The Grateful Kiss

Watch for the kiss in this gospel story:

LUKE 7.36-50

A very strictly religious man invited Jesus to dinner. Jesus accepted the invitation, arrived early with a host's gift, and sat down to eat. There was a woman of the red light district who got wind that Jesus was eating with Simon (the religious man). She got an alabaster jar of ointment and went to that house. (Perhaps she knew this Simon fella.) She sat down behind Jesus. Tears fell from her eyes onto the feet of Jesus. She used her long, black hair to dry his feet. Pouring the fragrant ointment on the Nazarene's feet, she began to kiss them. It was a strange scene—this woman of ill repute kissing a rabbi's feet.

Simon came into the room and was stunned at what he saw. At once he had doubts about the Teacher—allowing a loose woman to be so intimate with him. It was scandalous! Jesus saw the scowl on Simon's face. "Simon," said Jesus, "you want to hear a story?" "Sure," he said.

"Once upon a time there was a business man who had two men in debt to him. One of them owed him a thousand dollars; the other owed fifty thousand dollars. Neither of these men could pay back the debt. The business man was very kind. You know what he did?

He cancelled the debt of both men! Now, here's the question: Which one of those men would be the happiest?"

Simon said, "Well, of course the man who owed the $50,000 would be more excited than the other one." Jesus slapped him on the shoulder and said, "That's right."

Then Jesus motioned toward the woman. "Obviously, this woman is more excited to see me than you are. When I came in you didn't wash my feet, but she has. Look. She's washing my feet with her tears. And I don't remember you greeting me with the usual kiss of welcome. But look at her. She's still kissing me. And another thing: You forgot to anoint my head with oil. But she has anointed my feet with sweet smelling ointment."

"Do you get it, Simon? Her actions, which you think are out of place, clearly show a lot of love for me, which shows that she has received a lot of love from God. She's had more sins forgiven; therefore, her show of affection is more lavish. What she is doing is quite appropriate. She's expressing her love and gratitude to God for God's lavish mercy! You—well, you, I'm afraid to say, haven't shown much."

Then Jesus turned to the woman and said, "Miss, your sins are forgiven."

The other men around the table began to whisper behind his back, "What nerve! He claims to do what only God can do."

Then Jesus told the woman, "Your receptivity to grace has saved you. Go in peace."

A Sensual Scene

This is a very sensual story. You know the old phrase about "letting your hair down"? Well, this is obviously a slutty kind of woman because she is letting her hair down in public. And touching a man in public. She has brought ointment. The fragrance in the air might remind us of the lovers in the Song of Songs where ointments and spices are amorous accoutrements. The novelist Mary Gordon in a reflection on Luke's story says, "It is the most purely sensual moment in the Gospels."[49]

Watch her weep and wipe and rub and pour wet perfume and use her long luscious dark hair. Then—her lips—on his feet. Kissing. Kissing.

No wonder the host, a Pharisee, a strictly religious man, is offended at her behavior in his house. Furthermore, she seems to have a reputation outside the house.

What is this kissing all about?

Hospitality

The woman is identified as "a sinner." This implies she is a known prostitute. But Jesus stands up for her. He gently upbraids the host for his uppity attitude toward her. As is his usual modus operandi, Jesus uses a parable to make a sneak attack on self-righteousness. Before he knows what he's doing, the Pharisee has implicated himself as a "moral bully."[50]

Jesus points out to his host that he had not greeted Jesus with the usual courteous kiss that was common. But this woman had kissed him! She was being courteous and hospitable. Jesus graciously interpreted her kiss as a polite act of welcome.

Indeed hospitality is an important value in the Bible. In fact, it is so important that God brought down fire on the cities of Sodom and Gomorrah for their inhospitality to the visiting angels. (It wasn't about sex.)[51]

Forgiven

This is a story about forgiveness. She is not forgiven during the scene in Luke seven. She has already been forgiven. Paul Tillich, in a sermon, says:

> Jesus does not forgive the woman, but He declares that she *is* forgiven. Her state of mind and her ecstasy of love, show that something has happened to her. And nothing greater can happen to a human being than that he [or she] is forgiven.[52]

It is important to get the sequence right. So many people misunderstand this basic part of the Biblical message. *We do not repent in order to be forgiven. Rather, when we accept forgiveness we are led to repentance.*

> Forgiveness creates repentance.[53]

In the Bible, God always moves first.

Thanks

In a small village in northwestern Spain, a unique ritual is held each year on July 29, the feast day of Martha, sister to Lazarus, who was raised from the dead by Jesus. The ritual celebrates the lives of people who have been spared from death after a serious illness or accident the previous year. The "living dead" are put into coffins and carried in a procession around town. Some people participate in the procession to give thanks for the recovery of family members. The origins of this ritual, which stems from medieval times, are unknown.[54]

There are many ways to express thanks. The woman in Luke seven did it by kissing the feet of Jesus. How do you do it? How do you express your gratitude for grace? Saying prayers? Participating in worship? Doing what you can to help others? Giving money to causes that advocate for the weak or doing hands-on work with the poor? The 13th century Christian mystic Meister Eckhart said "If the only prayer you said in your whole life was *Thank you*, that would suffice."

The great 20th century theologian Karl Barth wrote:

> *Charis* always demands the answer of *eucharistia*. Grace and gratitude belong together like heaven and earth. Grace evokes gratitude like the voice an echo. Gratitude follows grace like thunder follows lightning.[55]

According to the Biblical narrative, one of the signs of estrangement from reality is ingratitude. In the first chapter of his correspondence with the Christians in Rome the first Christian theologian diagnoses the human dilemma and cites the lack of gratitude as a cause of our self-alienation and self-defeating behavior. Paul says:

> Ever since the creation of the world God's eternal power and divine nature, invisible though they are, have been understood and seen through the things God has made. So they are without excuse; for though they knew God, they *did not* honor God as God or *give thanks* [εὐχαριστέω – eucharisteō] to God, but they became futile in their thinking, and their senseless minds were darkened (Romans 1.20-21, NRSV).

Noting the positive, sanctifying power of gratitude, Paul writes to Timothy and says,

> Everything is good because God has created everything good. Nothing in nature is to be rejected, as long as it is received *with thanksgiving* (1 Timothy 4.4).

Dr. Luke tells about the time ten people with leprosy come to Jesus asking for healing. Jesus tells them to go the health department (the priest) and they will be healed and get a certificate of health. All ten take off. But one returns to thank Jesus for his healing power. Jesus says that this one man's faith has made him well (*sozo*).

The Greek word *sozo* can mean "well" or "whole" or "saved." Jesus seems to be saying that this one man isn't just physically healed from leprosy, but has received a kind of spiritual wholeness that the other nine have not received. The only difference is his expression of gratitude. There is healing power in thankfulness.

The *kiss of gratitude* speaks of wholeness of being. The Bible raises gratitude to the level of a virtue to be practiced. It is a virtue connected with faith, forgiveness, and hospitality. The woman kissing the feet of Jesus could not hold back her gratitude. Radical gratitude pushes us to do things that are beyond embarrassment. It takes us out of ourselves, transcending the bondage of the ego.

Healthy submission

When you meet the Pope you're supposed to kiss his hand as an expression of reverence. In ancient times one would kiss the feet of a king or queen.

In the second Psalm, David portrays the coronation of a new king.

> I will tell of the decree of the LORD: The LORD said to me, "You are my son; today I have begotten you" (Ps. 2.7, NRSV).

The words, "This day I have begotten you," meant to refer to the coronation ritual, have of course been picked up by Christians as a reference to Christ, the "only begotten one." In Psalm two David uses the word "son" to refer to the king. A king of Israel was called the "son of God."

As the Psalm progresses, David warns other earthly rulers to take notice of God's king on earth. David says:

> Now therefore, O kings, be wise;
>   be warned, O rulers of the earth.
> Serve the LORD with fear,
>   with trembling kiss his feet,
> or he will be angry, and you will perish in the way;
>   for his wrath is quickly kindled. (Psalm 2.11-12, NRSV)

To kiss the feet of the LORD (by kissing the king's feet) was a sign of obeisance. Isn't that what the sinful woman in Luke seven is doing? Along with all the other meanings of her kisses, isn't she expressing submission to Christ as the Messiah? (Messiah means "king.") Does that trouble you? After all, we live in a society where we are all "free." We submit to no one! We are all equal. We do not bow to another person! We kiss no one's ring—or feet!

I'm happy that a large portion of the Church has gotten over the passages where wives are told to *submit* to their husbands. It took us long enough to get over the Biblical verses that tell slaves to *submit to and obey* their masters. The Civil War is over. But the Patriarchal War is still being fought in some quarters. Any mention of *submission* makes us nervous.

But what about submitting to God? Are we over that too?

I remember hearing Christopher Hitchens in a debate with a Christian about the existence of God. Hitchens vehemently resisted any notion of a God because that meant (for him) that there was Someone with absolute authority over him. "I will not hand my freedom over to someone else," he said. Hitchens spoke for many people who reject the reality of God. A great many people have grown up in an oppressive religious environment in which the anger of God was constantly held over them as a threat; and moralistic preaching aimed at scaring people into heaven. No wonder they don't want "God" as part of their reality.

Unfortunately, the nature of Christian faith has been misconstrued in many times and places. A Puritanical version of the Biblical narrative has been offered as the real thing. And the Biblical meaning of "freedom" has been confused with the seventeenth and eighteenth century Enlightenment definition of "freedom."

The modern idea of "freedom" as absolute individual autonomy is rather new. But new does not equal true. The notion that freedom means I can do whatever I want to, and nobody can tell me what to do, sounds good. The Biblical story pushes back on that notion.

Theologian David Bentley Hart says, "We live now under the regime of negative liberty." By negative liberty he means the freedom that has no purpose; it is just freedom not to be told what to do.[56]

The fact is that the modern idea of freedom is unrealistic.

First, no one is free to do whatever they desire. I might "want to" be an NBA basketball player. But since I am only five foot ten inches tall and do not have the natural ability it takes to play basketball on that level, it doesn't matter how strong my "want-to" is; I cannot be an NBA player. In this case, my freedom is not attached to reality.

Second, if I hate people of a certain race and want to murder all of them, and set out to do so, my so-called "freedom" is not a good thing. Freedom disconnected from responsibility and accountability usually leads to behavior that is unacceptable.

Third, freedom to do what I want to which is not anchored in any larger purpose is like a boat drifting in the ocean.

Absolute freedom is a mythical idea; a superstition.

***

The narrative of the Bible affirms the value of freedom. The major story in the Hebrew Scriptures is the exodus of the Israelites from Egypt: liberation from slavery. This is a major theme in the Bible.

In Matthew's Gospel, Jesus is presented as the "new Moses." In Luke's Gospel the scene on the Mount of Transfiguration has Jesus talking to Moses and Elijah about his coming "exodus" – referring to his resurrection (exodus from death). Christian baptism analogous to "going through the water" of the Red Sea.

After Moses leads the people out of slavery, they go through the desert and face many trials. They arrive at Mount Sinai and receive the Ten Commandments. The journey through the desert has a purpose. It is to discipline the people and form them into a particular kind of community. The giving of the Law is for the purpose of instructing the people for their life together. All of this for giving the Israelites an identity as a covenant community.

Here is the point: their freedom has a purpose; the purpose is to form them into an intentional community of faith and service. The reason we are invited to *submit to God's sovereignty* is so that we can enter into the covenant relationship with God who calls us to trust Life, use our freedom for service to others (including the environment), and to experience the peace and fulfillment of being truly human—the way God created us to be.

We might understand this as a paradox: by submission to God we are truly free. Or we might see a logical pattern: by following our Maker's instructions we end up working like we are supposed to.

The Biblical idea of "freedom" is based on the assumption that life has a purpose and a meaning. To be free means to be find that purpose and live within it. Biblical freedom is participation in the peace we were made to be part of.

I quote David Bentley Hart again:

> True freedom is the realization of a complex nature in its proper ends, both natural and supernatural; it is the power of a thing to flourish, to become ever more full what it is… One must believe there is a transcendent Goo toward which that

nature is oriented. To be fully free is to b joined to that end for which our natures were originally framed, and whatever separates us from that end—including even our own personal choices—is a form of bondage. We are free, that is to say, not because we can choose, but only when we have chosen well.[57]

I'll risk a homey illustration. A train may decide it wants to be "free," and jumps off the tracks. Is it then free?

Perhaps we all know someone who has "found their calling," and is happy and fulfilled in their work because they feel like they are doing what they are "supposed" to be doing. Using Biblical language I would say of that person: I'm happy for you. You have kissed the feet of Jesus. You have found freedom: you are doing what you were "supposed" to do. Good for you.

Kissing the feet of Jesus is a picture being liberated by submission to the God who knows and loves us. God wants us to be free from illusion and self-destruction. Another word for that is *salvation.* The Biblical story of freedom is one that places us in a web of interrelationships which call us to creativity, accountability, mutual care, continual maturation, and authenticity.

The prostitute who heard the voice of God calling to her through the person of Jesus was set free from her degrading work by attaching herself to the cause of one who loved her instead of exploiting her. By following him she found freedom.

The Recap

Luke's story of the "loose woman" who has been loosed from her guilt and shame by the love of Jesus is an example of the core message of the Christian Scriptures.

The Bible…

- gives us examples of the way the grace of God transforms lives

- teaches that hospitality—a welcoming spirit—is a major virtue; and in doing so, rejects any exclusive form of spirituality

- emphasizes God's initiative in any process of healing, freedom, or salvation

- lifts up gratitude as a basic virtue for the fulfillment of our humanity

- presents the idea of submission to God as the way to authentic freedom, happiness, and fulfillment

- teaches that accepting God's forgiveness is the way to fall in love with God and live in intimacy with God

Chapter Seven

The Kiss of Grief

There is a story told by rabbis about a rabbi who is teaching a young student. They read from Deuteronomy 6.6: *And these words which I command thee this day shall be upon thy heart.* The student asks, "Why are we told to put these words upon our heart? Why are we not told to place them in our heart?" The teacher says, "It is not within our power to place the divine teachings directly in our heart. All that we can do is place them on the surface of the heart so that when the heart breaks they will drop in."[58]

There are many stories of heartbreak in the Bible. The Christian Scriptures addresses both the external and the internal realities of life. The Biblical narrative is about historical events and psychological events. What goes on around us and what goes on within us are both concerns of the God of Scripture.

The people who heard Jesus teach were living at a time when various philosophies were being taught. One such philosophy was Stoicism. Still to this day we hear the principles of the ancient Stoic teachers espoused, such as, "Keep a stiff upper lip." Or, "Grin and bear it." Or, "Que sera, sera—whatever will be, will be."

The Stoics offered a way to respond to life's troubles with serenity and confidence. One of their chief teachings was: *It's not what happens to you that counts; it's how you respond to what happens to you.* The Stoic philosophy has been revived in our time through the psychological school of thought known as Cognitive Therapy.

Aaron Beck and Albert Ellis both helped establish Cognitive Therapy as a mainline approach to psychotherapy. I can testify to the effectiveness of cognitive "restructuring" as a way to gain more personal peace. When I was in my thirties I gobbled up a host of books written by Albert Ellis. It was during a period of my life when I was trying to overcome debilitating anxiety and depression. Ellis' approach to re-educating my way of thinking was one of the main factors in my emotional journey of healing. The Stoic philosophy and the use of it by modern psychotherapists have much to offer in way of positive principles to live by.

Christian theology and Stoicism have some things in common. But there are important differences too.[59] The Stoic approach to life tends to be *unemotional.* The Stoics were hard-nosed rationalists. They urged a life of head-over-heart; reason over emotions; thinking over feeling; hardness over softness; guardedness over vulnerability. And there's the rub. The Biblical story values vulnerability.

Kisses in Miletus

St. Paul had lived in Ephesus for around three years (in the time frame of 52-57 CE). He was forced to leave because his teaching was rubbing some of the business men the wrong way. He journeyed through Asia Minor for a while, then decided to head back to Jerusalem. He sent word ahead to the elders (church leaders) in Ephesus to meet him in Miletus (about 50 miles south of Ephesus). It was an emotional scene. He reminisced about his time them and charged them to carry on the work. Then he delivered the sad news this would be the last time he would see them.

> When Paul had finished speaking, he knelt down and they prayed together. There was a lot of crying going on. One by

one they hugged and *kissed Paul*. They were so sad that they would not see him again (Acts 20.36-38).

There was no stoic attempt to hold back the tears. Followers of Jesus know the value of expressing emotional pain. After all, *Jesus wept* (John 11.35).

The Biblical story not only describes human vulnerability, but affirms the goodness of the emotional openness that some people would call weakness. Within the Christian Scriptures there is the recognition of the value of a holistic approach to human happiness. People are not just "minds," as if the rational aspect of our humanity is all that matters. People are affirmed in their wholeness—as rational, feeling, volitional, artistic, and somatic animals. We are told by Jesus to love God with all our *mind, heart, strength, and soul.* We are not just talking heads. Feelings matter. Emotions are not to be hidden or gunny-sacked.

Tears

The Protestant Reformer John Calvin warned against being detached from our feelings. He wrote:

> If all weeping is condemned, what shall we judge concerning the Lord himself, from whose body tears of blood trickled down? If all fear is branded as unbelief, how shall we account for that dread with which, we read, he was heavily stricken? If all sadness displeases us, how will it please us that he confesses his soul "sorrowful even to death"?[60]

The Apostle Paul wrote: *Cry with those who cry; and be happy for those who are happy* (Romans 12.15). In other words, sympathize and empathize. There is a ministry of tears—tears of joy and tears of sadness.

The Sunday after "9/11" I chose a Psalm as the basis of my sermon—Psalm 56.

> Have mercy on me, O God.
> My enemies are crushing me all day long…
> They wait in ambush,
> watching every move I make…
> God, throw them down!
> I know you will take care of them.
> You are with me through
> this journey of life.
> *You catch every one of my tears*
> *and keep them in your bottle.*
> My tears are not wasted.
> Therefore, I will trust you.
>
> (emphasis added)

I especially like the poetic thought of God *catching each one of our tears and saving them, so that they are not wasted.* Life is full of tears. The *kiss of grief* stands for all of our emotional pain and heartache. The Bible gives encouragement by its affirmation of the meaning of suffering and emotional distress.

In a letter to the congregation in Thessalonica Paul tells them *not to grieve as those who have no hope* (1 Thessalonians 4.13). Read carefully. He is not saying, "Do not grieve." Rather, he is saying that Christian grieving is hopeful grief. As Jesus-followers, our tears are not signs of despair. Our sorrow is held within the larger hope of "the resurrection of the body, and the life everlasting" (as the Apostles Creed puts it). For Christians, the *kiss of grief* is not the *kiss of death*.

God, Grief, & Guts

The *kiss of grief* is part of a gutsy theology. If we believe in God only with our intellect, but not with our gut, we have a truncated faith. The New Testament has a peculiar term for compassion or mercy. The original Greek New Testament has the word σπλάγχνα (splagchna), which in the old King James Version was rendered as "bowels." For example,

> Put on therefore, as the elect of God, holy and beloved, *bowels of mercies*, kindness, humbleness of mind, meekness, longsuffering. (Colossians 3:12, KJV)

There was the notion that mercy or compassion was deep in "the bowels" of a person. This is indeed gutsy faith.[61] Which is all to say that the deep reaches of the psyche are involved in the Bible's message.

In the well-known story The Good Samaritan, two religious figures (a priest and Levite) pass by the wounded man on the side of the road. Then,

> a certain Samaritan journeying came upon him and seeing him was filled with compassion [*esplagchnisthe*]... (Luke 10.33)

The Samaritan did not stop and calculate the risk. His action was not the result of an intellectual exercise. His gut told him to do something for the poor guy. The Samaritan was *moved* from deep within. He wasn't concerned with appearing to be emotional or sentimental. He took gutsy action to help the wounded human being before him.

The Bible is concerned with the whole person. Biblical religion is not about cerebral speculation concerning a Supreme Being. It is not an argument for God. The God of the Jewish and Christian Scriptures is revealed to us not only through our rational faculties, but also through our deep-down sensing of reality.

The 17th century mathematician and philosopher Blaise Pascal put it famously:

> The heart has its reasons of which reason knows nothing.[62]

The Christian faith is by no means anti-intellectual or irrational. The Church reveres "reason" as a blessed faculty for ordering life and understanding the world. Yet, the Biblical vision of life enlarges our capacity to celebrate our existence by enlarging "reason" to include transrational experiences that reach us through the *reasons of the heart* and the truth that tugs at our being in the bowels of our psyche. The narrative of the Bible dares to say that reality is not limited by human logic; that there is a Reason that is higher and deeper than that which comes from the firing of electrical impulses across our synapses.

Pepper in the Psalter

If you want a taste of the honest, holistic approach to human existence in the Bible, open the Book of Psalms. There you can sample and savor a generous variety of human emotion and feeling:

> grief,
> joy,
> fear,
> anger,
> rage,
> jealousy,
> envy,
> wonder,
> anxiety,
> loneliness,
> laughter,
> panic,
> gratitude,
> faith,
> doubt,
> despair,
> happiness,
> impatience,
> awe,
> distress,
> etc.

The Book of Psalms was both the hymnbook and prayer book of Jesus. In his dying moments he quoted it at least twice that we know of:

> *My God, my God, why have you forsaken me?* (Psalm 22)

Father, into your hands I commit my spirit. (Psalm 31)

The Church has historically used the Psalms for daily prayer. By praying the Psalms we express not only our desires and feelings, we also enter into the emotional lives of people in different circumstances from our own. For example, if in morning prayer you pray Psalm 22, it may not relate to your feelings or situation at the time you are praying. When the Psalmist says, "My God, my God, why have you forsaken me?" – those might not be the words you want to speak that morning. But it's not a waste of time, because there are other people all over the globe who are at that moment experiencing the emotions expressed in that Psalm. By praying it, you enter into their needs and join them in solidarity before God.

In this way the Psalter is a school of empathy. By reading/praying a Psalm in which someone is crying out in despair, we learn to enter into someone else's darkness. If we sing or chant a Psalm wherein a person is angry at the injustice in the world, we may "feel with" that person. Even when reading a Psalm where someone is seeking vengeance on his enemy, we can seek to share that person's hurt and rage at the violence done to him.

The Psalms may help open us up to our own fears and anxieties. It is sometimes difficult for us to admit that we don't "have it all together." We want others to see us as strong and stable all the time. But in order to empathize with others, and in order to risk loving those in need, we must be willing to open ourselves up and share our weaknesses honestly and willingly.

Vulnerability is part of love. Simon & Garfunkel's song "I Am a Rock" expresses this truth:

>Don't talk of love…
>…If I never loved, I never would have cried

> I am a rock
> I am an island…
> …A rock feels no pain
> An island never cries.[63]

The Book of Psalms refuses to let us live with the illusion of a life without tears or pain. We are neither rocks nor islands. We are vulnerable beings. Speaking or singing the words of Psalms will help us voice our vulnerability. The Psalter is peppered with non-Stoic expressions of weakness and panic. Even as I acknowledge the usefulness of some Stoic principles, I find a more authentic humanity in the Psalter.

God's grief

Can God feel? Does God have emotions? The Bible presents a God who emotes. For example, in the Letter to the Ephesians the writer says,

> Do not cause the Holy Spirit to grieve (4.30).

Really? We can cause God to experience grief? This is certainly not Aristotle's God—the Unmoved Mover.

In the Book of Exodus, the third chapter, God tells Moses that God hears the cry of the oppressed people of Israel under Pharaoh. God not only hears, God *knows* their suffering. This "knowing" is not just an intellectual knowledge. It is the same Hebrew word used when Adam *knows* Eve, and she conceives. By *knowing* the suffering of the Jews, God *participates* in their suffering—enters into it.

God feels.

The great twentieth century Jewish writer Abraham Joshua Heschel wrote a very influential book on the prophets in which he asserted that God's emotions described in Scripture are not merely anthropomorphic expressions, but point to something real in the essence of God. He writes:

> The Bible speaks in the language of man (sic). It deals with the problems of man, and its terms are borrowed from the vocabulary of the people. It has not coined many words, but it has given new meaning to borrowed words. The prophets had to use anthropomorphic language in order to convey [God's] nonanthropomorphic Being.[64]

Let's pause and meditate on that last sentence…

The Bible uses anthropomorphic language. This brings up a problematic fact. The only way we humans have to talk about God is with human language. But human language cannot really capture the essence of God. There is a sense in which we could say that everything we say about God is inaccurate. Our language is like a bucket used to carry water. (Let's say God is the water.) The problem is that our bucket has holes in the bottom. The water always leaks out. Our bucket is unable to contain the water.

Basically we have three options. First, we can talk about God as if what we say is literally true. That's fundamentalism. Second, we can talk about God with the realization that our words only point to the truth about God, but do not in any literal way tell the truth. Third, we can refuse to talk about God. Remain silent. (Some mystical forms of religion take this option.)

If we approach the Bible in the right attitude, the second option above is the best one. We must acknowledge that our God-talk is always symbolic, figurative, poetic, metaphorical, or whatever term you choose to use. Fundamentalists refuse to accept the metaphorical nature of Biblical language. They are stuck in the muck of literalism. The celebrity atheists of our time are stuck in the same place. Their criticisms of Biblical religion are based on literal interpretations of Biblical texts. They may have PhDs in astrophysics or some other field, but their theological and hermeneutical understanding is still in the kindergarten class of Sunday School.

Rabbi Heschel's quote above ends by talking about God's *nonanthropomorphic Being.* In other words, the God proclaimed in the Bible's Story is not a Large Man or a Super-sized Person. We use words that describe God that come from human feelings and activity. But those words point to a Reality that is qualitatively different from humans.

Our minds have to take a big leap in order to get over the false notion that God is just a bigger version of ourselves. This is a confusion that is hard to overcome because traditional Christian sentiment did not see the need to overcome it. But humans in the 21st century do not think about reality in the same way that 17th century folk did. People used to believe in demons, devils, fairies, etc. Most people no longer believe in such things (though a few do).

The fancy way to put this is that our consciousness has shifted. To say it more simply: We are much more down to earth, informed by science, not scared of ghosts, and no longer try to put spells on others. We know that "magic" is an illusion. We don't put faith in horoscopes. We don't perform rain dances. We no longer hunt down witches to drown or burn. (I'm speaking of the great majority of the human race; of course there are some people who consult mediums, follow their horoscope, believe in the Devil, etc.)

Because of our modern consciousness the idea of "a" God or Supreme Being who sits in the clouds glaring down at us no longer rings true to many people. And since those people have not learned to read the Biblical Narrative in an "updated" way, they throw the baby out with the bath water. The Bible makes no sense to them. It is simply an ancient book full of fairy tales, myths, outdated ideas, and downright cruel conceptions of God.

That is why I'm taking time to make clear that the human language of the Bible must be understood as *an anthropomorphic approach to a non-anthropomorphic Reality, namely, God.*

The best Christian theology asserts that the Bible bears witness to *God, not "a" God.* God is not an object, or one being alongside other beings. There is no "a" in front of "God." God is that from which everything comes. God is the basis of all reality. God is both inside all reality and outside of it at the same time. God is bigger than all of reality. *God is not "a" person. But—God is personal.* Neither our words nor our human concepts grasp God.

To refer to God as "he" is to point to the personal nature of God, but not to God as either male or "a" person. To call God "our Father" has nothing to do with gender. It is rather a metaphor for the all-encompassing love that we experience that comes from beyond ourselves, though we may feel it within ourselves. To speak of God as our Mother, our Friend, our Lover, etc., also works on a metaphorical level—to try and express a human experience of a phenomenon which we believe to be beyond human existence.

If we are to understand and appropriate the Biblical Story within the framework of 21st century consciousness, we have to be formed in literary imagination and theological subtlety. When in the 19th century the philosopher Nietzsche said, "God is dead," he was right. The God of the old consciousness has pretty much expired. But the God of our new consciousness is as fresh and alive as ever.

The Christian mystic, Meister Eckhart, prayed, "O God, rid me of God." A profound prayer. Eckhart was asking for the ability to let the God of his old understanding die so that the Real God could be experienced in his life. We must do likewise. There are old fashioned ideas of God that need to die. We would do well to give up the notion of the Big Man in the Sky. Or the Superman God who swoops down just in time to take away our pain, our disease, or our problem. There is no such God. It is hard to make this shift in our minds. Because when we give up that old God, a part of ourselves dies along with it. We need to be born again.

The trick is to look at the anthropomorphic language we use and translate it in our minds into something more sophisticated and real. It's a new way of reading. It takes practice.

God is spirit, and the words and images we use to describe God are approximations, drawn from our experience, to describe a Mystery.[65]

Rabbi Abraham Joshua Heschel described his "theology of pathos":

> [God] is also moved and affected by what happens in the world, and reacts accordingly. Events and human actions arouse in Him (sic) joy or sorrow, pleasure or wrath… He reacts in an intimate and subjective manner…Quite obviously in the biblical view, man's (sic) deeds may move Him, affect Him, grieve Him or, on the other hand, gladden and please Him. This notion that God can be intimately affected, that He possesses not merely intelligence and will,

but also pathos, basically defines the prophetic consciousness of God.[66]

The *kiss of grief* in Acts 20 is a report of human emotion, not divine. But because humans are made in the image of God, there is a correlation. It is not only the rationality of human beings that corresponds to God, but pathos as well. Rabbi Heschel implies such a connection when he writes, "For the biblical understanding of history, the idea of pathos is as central as the idea of man (sic) being an image of God is for the understanding of creation… The import of man raises him beyond the level of mere creature. He is a consort, a partner, a factor in the life of God."[67]

Heschel is echoing the Song of Songs with the "consort" language. The point is that the Bible is about a divine-human relationship—a romance. Both human emotion and divine emotion are part of the covenant between God and humans. Heschel expands on this point:

> The God of the prophets is not the Wholly Other, a strange, weird, uncanny Being, shrouded in unfathomable darkness, but the God of the covenant, Whose will they know and are called upon to convey. The God they proclaim is not the Remote One, but the One Who is involved, near, and concerned…What meets the biblical man [or woman] is a *transcendent relatedness.*"[68]

I want to hang on to that phrase—*transcendent relatedness.* A reminder: the word "transcendent" does not mean "far away." It means "different." God is not "way out there." God is near and can therefore "relate" to us. But God is Holy (qualitatively different); not a bigger version of us, but of a different category of being. God is Holy and Love at the same time. Different but close—close enough to relate—to love. Close enough to feel our pain. But different enough not to be sucked in by it. We encounter God as *transcendent relatedness.*

Passionate God

Theologian Rosemary Haughton says, "The poetry of passionate love is the accurate language of theology." It is no accident that Christians refer to the death of Jesus as the *Passion* of Christ. Passion means "suffering." Christianity is not an intellectual philosophy. It is a story of one who *suffers* for others. The meaning of the suffering and death of Jesus is love.

The cross is the symbol of God's vulnerability. In some sense "God was *in Christ* reconciling the world to Godself" (2 Corinthians 5.19). *God suffered* on our behalf. God took upon Godself the pain of our alienation—the ripped-apart-ness of the human condition. This is the scandal of the gospel.

The Holy Mystery of Love became vulnerable as a freely given gift. When Christ cried, "Why have you forsaken me?"—it was God sharing our existential aloneness. Using Christian symbolism we can speak of the *crucial* event this way: In the crucifixion, the Holy Trinity experienced an internal kiss of grief. The Father kissed the Son goodbye. God was split—as sometimes happens in birth. When at Golgotha the soldier thrust a spear into the side of Jesus, out came water and blood. A new creation was being born. The womb of God opened up on Golgotha; the scream of God was heard. And the cry of an infant creation pierced the veil.

The Recap

The Biblical vision of life not only with human history, but also with our inner histories. Each of us meets the Holy One in our psychic journeys. We come to know God not just with our mind, but with our feelings, our emotions, and our traumas.

The Bible…

- rejects the Stoic negation of emotional power

- sees our emotional vulnerability as a healthy part of our humanity

- honors pain and suffering as part of life's journey

- offers us emotional poetry and music that speaks to our human condition and functions as prayer, especially in the Book of Psalms

- gives us in the Psalms a means of entering into the suffering of others

- reveals God to be a caring, empathic Reality which may be symbolically imagined as a "person"

- warns against idolatry, which easily comes in the form of building a mental picture of a god who is like us, just bigger

- is full of poetry and symbolic language, which when taken literally, warps the message of the story

- asserts that in some mysterious way God has entered human history and taken on our pain and shame through the life and execution of Jesus of Nazareth

- narrates the story of Transcendent Being relating to the earth and its inhabitants; it tells of the Source (Creator) "who" is qualitatively different from the creation/creatures, yet present within and all around

Chapter Eight

The Cosmic Kiss

Psalm 85

A little known kiss in the Bible is found in Psalm 85. Here is the whole chapter from the New Revised Standard Version (adapted for inclusive language):

> [1] LORD, you were favorable to your land;
> you restored the fortunes of Jacob.
> [2] You forgave the iniquity of your people;
> you pardoned all their sin. *Selah*
> [3] You withdrew all your wrath;
> you turned from your hot anger.
> [4] Restore us again, O God of our salvation,
> and put away your indignation toward us.
> [5] Will you be angry with us forever?
> Will you prolong your anger to all generations?
> [6] Will you not revive us again,
> so that your people may rejoice in you?

⁷ Show us your steadfast love, O LORD,

    and grant us your salvation.

⁸ Let me hear what God the LORD will speak,

    for God will speak peace to God's people,

    to God's faithful, to those who turn to God in their hearts.

⁹ Surely God's salvation is at hand for those who fear God,

    that God's glory may dwell in our land.

¹⁰ Steadfast love and faithfulness will meet;

    righteousness and peace will kiss each other.

¹¹ Faithfulness will spring up from the ground,

    and righteousness will look down from the sky.

¹² The LORD will give what is good,

    and our land will yield its increase.

¹³ Righteousness will go before the LORD,

    and will make a path for God's steps.

Did you see the "kiss"? Let me set the stage.

You'll remember that the city of Jerusalem was attacked and destroyed in the year 586 BCE. Virtually all the Jews were marched out of town, some 900 miles to the city of Babylon. Living in exile was a shocking experience. Everyone lost their home, their place of worship, their culture, their symbols, and their sense of identity. A psalm written during the exile says, "How can we sing our songs to our God in a foreign land?" (Psalm 137.4) The Jewish people were devastated. But after the fall of Babylon to the Persian King Cyrus the Great in 539 BCE, exiled Judeans were permitted to return to Palestine.

Psalm 85 was written shortly after they returned to Jerusalem. The first three verses look back at God's deliverance from exile. Notice the words *restored, forgave, pardoned.*

> ¹ Lord, you were favorable to your land;
>   you *restored* the fortunes of Jacob.
> ² You *forgave* the iniquity of your people;
>   you *pardoned* all their sin. Selah
> ³ You withdrew all your wrath;
>   you turned from your hot anger.

The return from exile was seen by the post-exilic prophets as a sign that Israel had been forgiven its sins that sent them to the foreign land. For example Second Isaiah says:

> Comfort, O comfort my people,
>   says your God.
> Speak tenderly to Jerusalem,
>   and cry to her
> that she has *served her term*,
>   that her *penalty is paid* (Isaiah 40.1-2, NRSV).

So, Psalm 85 begins by celebrating God's mercy in forgiving their sins and bringing them back to their homeland.

The Grammar of Salvation

But being back home again hasn't solved all their problems. Salvation is an ongoing process. In a sense they have been 'saved'; they are home again. Salvation has something to do with a homecoming. But their salvation is not complete.

I feel the same way about myself. Don't you? I believe the Good News (gospel) that Jesus of Nazareth announced to the world through his words and actions. I believe I am 'saved.' But not fully. I have a sense of being forgiven and accepted into God's family. But I'm still a sinner and I still cannot accept myself fully. There is more to come.

Salvation is all 'tensed up.' That is, salvation has a past, a present, and a future tense. Something has already happened. Jesus was born, lived as a Jew in the Middle East, he died, and he was resurrected. That is past tense. Christians see those past events as saving events. God has already done something decisive through Jesus. To profess the Christian faith is to profess that Jesus Christ *is Lord—already.*

And there is a present tense to salvation. I am *being saved.* The classic term for this process is 'sanctification' – the ongoing work of the Holy Spirit in our lives. God is not finished with us yet! Thank goodness! The Spirit is *right now* working on you and on me. Spirit is helping our faith evolve into a more mature faith. Spirit's inner work on us is like an inner purgatory as the Spirit purges us of immaturity, egotism, selfishness, arrogance, etc. Salvation is happening now, in the present tense.

But there is also a future tense. (It ain't over till the fat angel sings.) What Jesus started will be finished in the future. And this is the situation Israel finds itself in as we read Psalm 85. (Of course this is still pre-Christ, but they are experiencing the 'tense' nature of redemption.) Look at the next few verses to hear their ongoing cry for deliverance.

> 4 Restore us again, O God of our salvation,
>   and put away your indignation toward us.
> 5 Will you be angry with us forever?

> Will you prolong your anger to all generations?
> 6 Will you not revive us again,
>   so that your people may rejoice in you?
> 7 Show us your steadfast love, O Lord,
>   and grant us your salvation.

In other words, "Lord, you have delivered us from exile. But that's not enough. Keep on delivering us."

Then, at verse 8, someone steps up and begins to reassure the people that God isn't finished with them yet.

> ⁸ Let me hear what God the LORD will speak,
>   for God will speak peace to God's people,
>   to the faithful, to those who turn to the LORD
>   in their hearts.
> ⁹ Surely God's salvation is at hand for those
>   who fear God,
>   that God's glory may dwell in our land.

Great news! "God's salvation is at hand. God's glory will dwell in our land." Do not despair. God isn't finished yet.

Coming Together

Drum roll, please.

Here is what we have been waiting for: *The Kiss.*

> 10 Steadfast love and faithfulness will meet;

> *righteousness and peace will kiss each other.*
> 11 Faithfulness will spring up from the ground,
>   and righteousness will look down from the sky.
> 12 The Lord will give what is good,
>   and our land will yield its increase.
> 13 Righteousness will go before God,
>   and will make a path for God's steps.

Notice how everything is 'coming together.' Two entities *meet*. Two entities *kiss*. One entity *springs up* from the ground. Another entity *looks down* from the sky. Things separated are coming together.

This is a *big* vision. The 16th century reformer John Calvin says in his commentary on this Psalm:

> *The springing of truth out of the earth,* and *the looking down of righteousness from heaven,* without doubt imply, that truth and righteousness will be universally diffused, as well above as beneath, so as to fill both heaven and earth. It is not meant to attribute something different to each of them, but to affirm in general, that there will be no corner of the earth where these qualities do not flourish.[69]

The kiss we are looking at envisions a world of perfect harmony. The great divide between *is* and *ought* is overcome. The world will be the way it *ought* to be. Martin Luther King's dream will come true. The nightmare of injustice, cruelty, hatred, bigotry, greed, and exploitation will cease and desist. John Lennon's song will become reality. Can you imagine such a world? Well, the Bible does.

Old Testament scholar Robert Alter makes these comments on this passage:

> *Kindness and truth.* The two terms of the familiar hendiadys.

> *Hesed we'emet* ("steadfast loyalty") are separated and turned into figures, along with another pair, justice and peace, in a kind of allegory of the ideal moment when God's favor is restored to the land.
>
> *Justice and peace have kissed.* This bold metaphor focuses the sense of an era of perfect loving harmony.[70]

New Testament scholar N.T. Wright points out that the Bible doesn't talk about people "going to heaven." Rather, it consistently paints a picture of a "new heaven and a new earth." The idea of new heavens and a new earth is explicitly noted in Isaiah 65:17; 66:22; 2 Peter 3:13; and Revelation 21:1.

Wright writes:

> Heaven, in the Bible, is not a future destiny but the other, hidden, dimension of our ordinary life—God's dimension, if you like. God made *heaven and earth*; at the last he will remake both and *join them together* forever. And when we come to the picture of the actual end in Revelation 21-22, we find not ransomed souls making their way to a disembodied heaven, but rather the new Jerusalem coming down from heaven to earth, *uniting the two* in a lasting embrace.[71] (emphasis added)

Apocalyptic Nuptials

Further, this great uniting is set forth in the last book of the Bible as a *marriage!* When you attend a wedding you know what is going to happen at the very end of the ceremony. The clergy will say something like, "You may now seal the covenant with a kiss." The two people kiss, and we all applaud. This is what happens at the end of the Bible—in Revelation 21. The New Jerusalem comes down out of heaven "like a bride adorned for her husband." This symbolizes the Church's wedding with Christ. In a more general way it symbolizes the uniting of the whole cosmos.

The kiss in Psalm 85.10 anticipates the final kiss when perfect harmony is established at the wedding (coming together) of all things. Of course this has been the plan all along according to the gospel. St. Paul says in the Letter to the Ephesians:

> With wisdom and insight God has revealed to us the mystery of God's dream for the world which was glimpsed in Christ; namely, the ultimate goal of history is *uniting all things* in Christ, things in heaven and on earth (Ephesians 1.8-10).

The Maker of the universe—the One who lit the fuse for the Big Bang—had a plan from the beginning. Our lives are dignified by having a part in that plan. It is not a plan in which everything is predetermined. We humans have freedom to make choices and even mess things up to a certain extent. The evolutionary process takes its own turns and twists without micromanagement. But the outcome is to be determined by the sovereign God.

At the end of history as we know it there will be a wedding. Everything will be *joined together* in holy matrimony. The kiss of Psalm 85.10 is the preview of the coming 'attraction' and consummation.

All shall be well

Don't think that this is just some ethereal concept. No, the reality of the final kiss means that life matters; the choices we make matter; life has meaning and purpose—we are not part of a cosmic accident. It also implies that all of the injustices of human history will somehow be set right. The pain will be redeemed. All tragedies will turn from tearful dissonance to beautiful harmony.

The fourteenth century English mystic, Julian of Norwich, gave us a fetching vision of the end. She wrote:

> But Jesus, who in this vision informed me of all that is needed by me, answered with these words and said: "It was necessary that there should be sin; but all shall be well, and all shall be well, and all manner of thing shall be well."[72]

The British physicist John Polkinghorne expresses his belief this way:

> Final fulfillment, though arrived at through the contingencies of history, is guaranteed by the steadfast love of a God ceaselessly at work within that history, whose benevolent intention will not ultimately be thwarted.[73]

I do not have enough faith to be an atheist. The cosmos displays order and wisdom. I don't believe the movement of the universe (everything is in motion) lacks purpose. It seems to be moving *toward something.*

It is hard for me to believe mind/consciousness has evolved from a mindless universe. The Divine Mind behind our world is the Logos

(Reason) revealed in Jesus. It is a Mind that creates with a "purpose in mind." Life is going somewhere.

Why does life evolve? Because there is a *push* for life that comes from a life-giving Source; a *push* that is encoded within the process. The *push* for life is no accident. The order of our cosmos is not arbitrary. I think we intuitively know this is true.

The Biblical message muses on this great drama of life. The Scriptures "kiss and tell." The Biblical narrative presents the ordered reality we are part of as being guided by a transcendent power. The story is told in the form of myth, poetry, parable, oracle, saga, apocalypse, historical fiction, short story, biography, correspondence, etc. But the story also revolves around real historical events and personages in actual geographical locations. The Bible is a work of art—an epic story sculpted out of history, religion, politics, and social movements.

The Bible acknowledges the mess the world is in. There is betrayal, evil, and tragedy. Yet, there is also something urging us on toward goodness, healing, and hope. Some people think it naïve to trust in an unseen power at work in history and the natural order—a power that desires our personal wholeness and a larger cosmic wholeness. Other people think it wise to trust in such a power.

The Bible presents the option of aligning our lives with a hidden, incomprehensible, infinite Personality that wills our happiness. The Narrative of the Christian Bible focuses on a particular people—the Jews—and a specific person—the Jewish man, Jesus of Nazareth, as clues to the meaning of human history. The sacred texts of the Christian faith assert that as foolish as it may seem, in the Jew named Jesus, God has kissed the world.

The Recap

Psalm 85 tells of the Jewish hope after returning from exile. The nation has come home, but there is much to be done to rebuild. The restoration has just begun. David gives encouragement by assuring the people that everything will come together. There will be a *kiss*, a reunion, heaven and earth will join as partners and become one. I have taken this vision within history as a prototype of the final eschatological harmony envisioned by the Biblical story. It ends with the wedding of all things.

The Bible…

- narrates redemptive memory (the past), quotidian spirituality (the present), and eschatological promise (the future)

- anticipates a victorious climax to the life of the universe: a "new heaven and a new earth"

- offers a vision of an eternal Goodness which will redeem all suffering and shame

- tells of a God who is engaged with the world

- invites everyone to the Wedding

Epilogue

An ancient Norwegian legend says that when God creates a human soul, God plants a kiss on it, and it remains there forever, leaving a deep memory of the One who bestowed it.

Each one of us is living in a sacred drama in which the Eternal One is luring us back to Its embrace—to that first kiss upon our soul.[74]

This is what the Bible calls *the Gospel* (Good News). God is always inviting us into a love affair. When we think the news is too good to be true, we're like someone standing under Niagara Falls with a teacup, worrying that it won't be enough.[75]

The Bible is about our desire to be kissed—a desire that God wants to fulfill. With kisses sweeter than wine.

NOTES

[1] "A fuller edition," a poem by Joseph Lilienthal. Wallace and Frances Rice, eds., *The Humbler Poets (Second Series); A Collection of Newspaper and Periodical Verse 1885 to 1910* (BiblioBazaar, 2009).
[2] Tom Gledhill in his commentary, *The Message of the Song of Songs* (Downers Grove, IL: Inter-Varsity Press, 1994), p. 171.
[3] Wayne Teasdale, *The Mystic Heart* (New World Library 1999), p. 222.
[4] Roger Housden, *for lovers of god everywhere: Poems of the Christian Mystics* (Carlsbad, CA: Hay House, Inc., 2009), p. 6. This selection translated by Daniel Ladinsky.
[5] Ibid., Housden, p. 16. Translation by Regis J. Armstrong or Ignatius C. Brady in *Francis and Clare: The Complete Works* (Paulist Press, 1982).
[6] Ibid., Housden, p. 86. Translation by Ellen L. Babinsky.
[7] Quoted by Matthew Fox, *One River, Many Wells* (NY: Jeremy Tarcher/Penguin, 2000), 33.
[8] Paula D'arch, *Seeking with All My Heart* (New York: The Crossroad Publishing Company, 2003), p. 52.
[9] From an interview in *The Sun*, July 2015, p. 9. Fr. Fox has a Ph.D. in the history and theology of spiritualities from the Institut Catholique de Paris.
[10] Daniel Ladinsky, *A Year with Hafiz: Daily Contemplations* (Ne York: Penguin Books, 2010), 382.
[11] *Bernard of Clairvaux on the Song of Songs I*, trans. by Kilian Walsh, OCSO (Kalamazoo, MI: Cistercian Publications, 1981), p. 10.
[12] Blaise Arminjon, *The Cantata of Love*, trans. by Nelly Marans (San Francisco: Ignatius Press, 1988), p. 57.
[13] Dietrich Bonhoeffer, *Life Together* (New York: Harper & Row, 1954).
[14] "Wilderness," *The Complete Poems of Carl Sandburg* (Harcourt Brace Iovanovich Inc., 1970).
[15] From *Leviathan*.
[16] From *Discourse on the Origin and Foundations of Inequality Among Men*.
[17] See *The Economy of Nature and the Evolution of Sex*.
[18] Rabbi Jonathan Sacks, *Essays on Ethics* (New Milford, CT: Maggid Books & The Orthodox Union, 2016), *10*.

[19] *The Way Things Are,* ed. Phil Cousineau (Berkeley: University of California Press, 2003), 145-6.
[20] Quoted by Robert Cardinal Sarah, (San Francisco: Ignatius Press, 2017), 145.
[21] C.S. Lewis, *The Four Loves* (New York: Harcourt, Brace, 1960).
[22] Jess Blumberg, Smithsonian.Com, October 23, 2007.
[23] Mary Margaret Funk, *Thoughts Matter* (New York: Continuum, 1999), 78.
[24] I do not know the origin of this story. I received it in an email from Adrienne Rexroad.
[25] From *Twilight of the Idols*, 1888. "Obl.S.B." means that Lucie is an Oblate of Saint Benedict.
[26] Found in *Prayer in All Things* (Liturgical Press, 2004).
[27] These examples are taken from Martin Laird's book, *Into the Silent Land: A Guide to the Christian Practice of Contemplation* (Oxford University Press, 2006), chapter three.
[28] The Dalai Lama, *Healing Anger* (Ithaca, NY: Snow Lion Publications, 1997), 78.
[29] http://www.visitationmonasteryminneapolis.org/2013/11/tonglen-a-meditation-tool-to-transform-suffering/
[30] *The Intimate Merton: His Life from His Journals,* ed. Patrick Hart and Jonathan Montaldo (HarperSanFrancisco, 1999), 130.
[31] Fyodor Dostoevsky, *The Brothers Karamazov,* Trans. by Richard Pevear and Larissa Volokhonsky (New York: Alfred A. Knopf; Everyman's Library, 1992), Chapter Five.
[32] Paul Tillich, *The Shaking of the Foundations* (New York: Charles Scribner's Sons, 1955), pp. 161-162.
[33] Fred Rogers received his Master of Divinity Degree from the Pittsburg Theological Seminary and was ordained as a Presbyterian Clergy in 1963. He was commissioned to a ministry to families through public media.
[34] Rabbi Jonathan Sacks, Ibid., 113-114.
[35] I have paraphrased a story from an article by Richard J. Mouw in the May 15, 2007 edition of *Christian Century.*
[36] Reported in *The Week*, June 10, 2016.
[37] *The Week*, March 23, 2018.
[38] Rabbi Jonathan Sacks, Ibid., 110.
[39] The Dalai Lama, Archbishop Desmond Tutu, with Douglas Abrams, *The Book of Joy* (New York: Avery, 2016), pp. 182f.
[40] David Bentley Hart, *The Experience of God* (New Haven: Yale University Press, 2013), 70-71.
[41] *The Way Things Are,* ed. Phil Cousineau (Berkeley: University of California Press, 2003), 150-1.

[42] Quoted by David Bentley Hart, Ibid., 305.
[43] Ian Hutchinson, *Monopolizing Knowledge: A Scientist refutes religion-denying, reason-destroying scientism* (Belmont MA: Fias Publishing, 2011), 1.
[44] Ibid., 60.
[45] Ibid., 231.
[46] John Walton, *The Lost World of Genesis One* (Downers Grove, IL: IVP Academic, 2009), 114-15.
[47] St. John Paul II, *Go in Peace: A Gift of Enduring Love* (Chicago: Loyola Press, 2003), 92-93.
[48] St. Augustine, Homily 7 on the First Letter of John, par. 8.
[49] Mary Gordon, *Reading Jesus: A Writer's Encounter with the Gospels* (New York: Pantheon Books, 2009), 36.
[50] Mary Gordon, Ibid.
[51] See: http://www.huffingtonpost.com/rev-patrick-s-cheng-phd/what-was-the-real-sin-of_b_543996.html; see: https://www.onfaith.co/onfaith/2010/12/08/homosexuality-in-sodom-and-gomorrah/9051; see: https://baptistnews.com/article/the-sins-of-sodom-and-gibeah-the-lgbt-issue-part-9/#.Wa7pOtOGN0s.
[52] Paul Tillich, *The New Being,* (New York: Charles Scribner's Sons, 1955), 7.
[53] Ibid., 9.
[54] *Christian Century,* August 30, 2017.
[55] Karl Barth, *Church Dogmatics: The Doctrine of Reconciliation* (London: T&T Clark, 2004), 41-42.
[56] David Bentley Hart, "Christianity, Modernity, and Freedom," in *The Hidden and the Manifest* (Grand Rapids, MI: William B. Eerdmans Publishing Company, 2017), p. 322.
[57] Ibid., p. 313.
[58] Adapted from *Reasoned Faith: Essays On the Interplay of Faith and Reason,* ed. Frank T. Birtel (Crossroad, 1993).
[59] See: Alexis Trader, *Ancient Christian Wisdom and Aaron Beck's Cognitive Therapy: A Meeting of Minds* (New York: Peter Lang, 2012). See also: Mark R. McMinn, *Cognitive therapy techniques in Christian counseling* (Eugene, OR: Wipf & Stock, 2007).
[60] Quoted by Michelle Sanchez, "Dethroning the Idols," *Christian Century,* August 30, 2017, 33.
[61] Merriam-Webster: "bowel": *2 archaic* : the seat of pity, tenderness, or courage —usually used in plural.
[62] Blaise Pascal, *Pensees,* Trans. A. J. Krailsheimer, (London: Penguin Books, 1966). par. 423.

[63] From the album "Sounds of Silence," 1966.
[64] Abraham Joshua Heschel, *The Prophets: Two Volumes in One* (Hendrickson, Peabody, MA, 1962), II, 56.
[65] *The Inclusive Hebrew Scriptures, Volume III: The Writings* (Walnut Creek, CA: AltaMira Press, 2004), p. xxx. A project of Priests For Equality.
[66] Heschel, Ibid., II, 4.
[67] Ibid., II, 6.
[68] Ibid., II, 7 (emphasis added).
[69] John Calvin, *Commentary on the Book of Psalms, Vol. III,* Trans. James Anderson (Grand Rapids: Wm. B. Eerdmans Publishing Co., 1949), 376.
[70] Robert Alter, *The Book of Psalms: A Translation with Commentary* (New York: W.W. Norton & Company, 2007).
[71] N. T. Wright, *Surprised By Hope: Rethinking Heaven, the resurrection, and the Mission of the Church* (HarperOne, 2008), 19.
[72] Julian of Norwich, *Showings*, Chapter 27.
[73] John Polkinghorne, *The Faith of a Physicist* (Minneapolis: Fortress Press, 1996), 66.
[74] Susan R. Pitchford, *God in the Dark: Suffering and Desire in the Spiritual Life* (Collegeville, Minnesota: Liturgical Press, 2011), 56.
[75] Ibid., 23.

Printed in Great Britain
by Amazon